GREY OWL *and* ME

GREY OWL *and* ME

STORIES FROM THE TRAIL AND BEYOND

HAP WILSON

Illustrated by Hap Wilson *and* Ingrid Zschogner

NATURAL HERITAGE BOOKS
A MEMBER OF THE DUNDURN GROUP
TORONTO

Copy Editor: Allison Hirst
Design: Jennifer Scott
Printer: Webcom

Library and Archives Canada Cataloguing in Publication

Wilson, Hap, 1951-
Grey Owl and me : stories from the trail and beyond / by Hap Wilson ;
        illustrated by Hap Wilson and Ingrid Zschogner.

Includes bibliographical references.
ISBN 978-1-55488-732-3

1. Wilson, Hap, 1951-. 2. Outdoor life--Canada. 3. Grey Owl, 1888-1938. 4. Environmentalists--Canada--Biography. 5. Outfitters (Outdoor recreation)--Canada--Biography. 6. Park rangers--Canada--Biography. I. Zschogner, Ingrid II. Title.

GV191.52.W54A3 2010   796.5092   C2009-907449-4

1   2   3   4   5   14   13   12   11   10

We acknowledge the support of the **Canada Council for the Arts** and the **Ontario Arts Council** for our publishing program. We also acknowledge the financial support of the **Government of Canada** through the **Canada Book Fund** and **The Association for the Export of Canadian Books**, and the **Government of Ontario** through the **Ontario Book Publishers Tax Credit program**, and the **Ontario Media Development Corporation**.

Care has been taken to trace the ownership of copyright material used in this book. The author and the publisher welcome any information enabling them to rectify any references or credits in subsequent editions.

J. Kirk Howard, President

Printed and bound in Canada.
www.dundurn.com

Front cover: (top) Grey Owl with beaver kit at Lake Ajawaan, Saskatchewan, *circa* 1930s. *Courtesy of the Barry Penhale Collection*; (bottom) Hap Wilson. Photo by nine-year-old Alexa Wilson.

Back cover: Illustration by Ingrid Zschogner.

Dundurn Press
3 Church Street, Suite 500
Toronto, Ontario, Canada
M5E 1M2

Gazelle Book Services Limited
White Cross Mills
High Town, Lancaster, England
LA1 4XS

Dundurn Press
2250 Military Road
Tonawanda, NY
U.S.A. 14150

*This book is dedicated to those who are unafraid
to paddle their canoe against the current,
and who have found humour in all adversity*

TABLE OF CONTENTS

Part Three: Natura   **187**

THE CANADIAN SHIELD.

Ingrid Zschogner.

Should you ask me, whence these stories
Whence this legends and traditions,
With the odor of the forest,
With the dew and damp of meadows,
With the curling smoke of wigwams,
With the rushing of great rivers,
With their frequent repetitions,
As a thunder of the mountains?
I should answer, I should tell you,
"From the forests and the prairies,
From the land of the Ojibways,
From the land of the Dacotahs,
From the mountains, moors and fen-lands,
Where the heron, the Shuh-shuh-gah,
Feeds among the reeds and rushes.
I repeat them as I heard them
From the lips of Nawadaha,
The musician, the sweet singer."

— Introduction to "The Song of Hiawatha,"
1855, Henry Wadsworth Longfellow

GREY OWL:

SCOUNDREL OR CHAMPION?

A SHORT BIOGRAPHY

Born September 18, 1888, in Hastings, England, Archibald Stansfield Belaney was the son of a teenage bride and a reprobate father. Raised by two strict aunts, Archie fantasized early on about the true identity of his parents. Intertwining his love of animals and his fascination with the Canadian Indian, young Archie created an imaginary lineage as the Mexican-born son of a Scots outdoorsman and an Apache mother.

Becoming increasingly restless, Archie immigrated to Canada in 1906, at age seventeen, to work as a clerk in a Toronto department store, and to be close to his beloved Indians. He soon took the train north and was taken in by Temiskaming guide and trapper Bill Guppy, who taught him many outdoor skills. Archie found work as a chore boy at one of Dan O'Conner's lodges on Lake Temagami and befriended the Indians at Bear Island.

Archie was "adopted" by John Eguana, brother-in-law of Chief White Bear, and in 1910 married his niece Angele. He learned to speak Ojibwa phrases, and dropped his English accent. Armed with these newly acquired skills, Archie became adept at both trapping and guiding throughout the Temagami District.

Chief White Bear, Ned White Bear, and Michael Mathias were all great influences on Archie, teaching him the ways of the wilderness trail and how to paddle a canoe. Eguana called him "the young owl who sits taking everything in." Archie liked the cognomen and implemented the name Grey Owl for himself.

Only a year later, starting to drink heavily and yearn for his freedom, Archie abandoned his wife and newborn daughter, Agnes, and headed to Biscotasing, where he worked as a forest ranger for the next four years. He took a common-law Métis wife, Marie Gerard (1913–14), but she died of tuberculosis soon after giving birth to a son (Johnny). Archie led a troubled life in Bisco, often aggravating the authorities with his knife-throwing antics and heavy drinking.

In 1915 he joined the war effort as a sniper with the 13th Montreal Battalion, Black Watch infantry, and was shipped to France. He was wounded in the foot, and discharged with a disability pension. He had enlisted as unmarried, however, depriving his legal wife, Angele, of any government assistance.

In 1917 he married his childhood sweetheart, Ivy Holmes, to whom he had been reintroduced while recovering from his injuries at the home of his aunt in Hastings. Holmes divorced Archie after refusing to meet him in Canada.

When he returned to Canada, Archie continued to fine-tune his Indian lineage and characterizations by dying his hair and skin. Back in Temagami in 1925, he worked as a guide for Camp Keewaydin, once again taking up with Angele, who soon after had a second child, Flora.

Archie then met nineteen-year-old Gertrude Bernard, a Mattawa Iroquois who worked in the kitchen at Camp Wabikon. Archie Grey Owl was thirty-seven. Gertrude joined him on his trapping line in northern Quebec and talked him into changing his profession to writer/conservationist. Through her influence, Grey Owl began to think more deeply about the plight of the Canadian beaver and to publish his articles about wilderness life.

After he and "Pony," as Grey Owl called Anahareo, attempted to set up a beaver colony with two rescued beaver kits near Lac Temiscouta, Quebec, Archie's published stories became popular. His writings attracted the attention of the Dominion Parks Service, and Grey Owl and Anahareo were set up as park naturalists in 1931 in Manitoba's Riding Mountain National Park. The next year they moved to Ajawaan Lake in Prince Albert

National Park in Saskatchewan and set up a beaver colony with pet beavers Jellyroll and Rawhide. Grey Owl and Anahareo, not legally married, had a daughter (Shirley Dawn, 1932).

In his articles, books, and films, Grey Owl promoted conservation; from 1935 to 1937 Grey Owl successfully toured England and lectured, wearing traditional Native clothing. Only his aunts and a North Bay *Nugget* reporter knew of Owl's true identity, and they remained silent because of his success as an environmentalist. Anahareo soon tired of Owl's heavy drinking and mood swings on the tour and returned home to prospect in northern Canada.

Grey Owl then married Yvonne Perrier, a medical assistant from Ottawa, in 1936. After a heavy lecture tour, he returned to Lake Ajawaan (Beaver Lodge), where he died of pneumonia on April 13, 1938, at the age of fifty.

After his death, the North Bay *Nugget* announced Grey Owl's true identity — with global repercussions. Canadian Parks denounced him and publishers stopped distributing his books, but the general Canadian Native community stood by his conservation efforts. Posthumous recognition for his environmental work and poignant writing about the disappearing Canadian wilderness raised Archie Grey Owl's reputation as a great Canadian.

INTRODUCTION

I can't remember that I had any heroes when I was growing up. The male members of my immediately family were anything but high-quality role models, unless of course I was to follow a path of self-indulgence, narcissism, bigotry, and heavy drinking. I was running wild at fourteen, emulating a self-fashioned quasi-Native lifestyle whenever I ventured outside the confined box my parents tried to put me in. Sneaking out my bedroom window to sleep in a tepee in a replicated Indian stockade, hunting game with a homemade bow, and running through the woods dressed in a loincloth was not the typical agenda for a teenager who didn't even have a driver's licence yet. I learned how to speak Ojibwa phrases, and my Indian name — a self-appellation — was *pungashe neegig*, or "little otter."

I figured out how to tan hides using the brains of the animal to help scrub the grease off the pelts, ate groundhog meat, and learned to throw a tomahawk and a knife. Evenings were spent counting coup on the neighbour kids by taunting them to chase me; I could lose them in the woods by hiding under stumps, burying myself in leaves just to see how close they would walk by without my being discovered. I watched almost no TV and read few books except for the odd adventure story, such as Farley Mowat's *Two Against the Wilderness* and Jack London's *Call of the Wild*; classic adventure tales, the romance of the wilderness, of primordial landscapes and a lifestyle far removed from the one I was supposed to conform to. I got lost in those books. There were no heroes, just landscapes and a way of life I aspired to create for myself. I could already live off the land, navigate through the woods without a compass, and had embarked on several lengthy canoe expeditions by the time I was halfway through high school.

When my reclusive math teacher, Mr. McConaghy, introduced me to a map of Temagami, he also handed me a book entitled *Men of the Last Frontier*. It was written by a Canadian author with the unlikely name of Grey Owl.

"He was really an Englishman," my teacher said.

"He wanted to be an Indian, like you, and wrote about his experiences masqueraded as an Indian," he went on, talking as if he knew him personally. I was captured.

"I met him once," he said, "When I was young, in Toronto, and he was on the speaking circuit, talking about Temagami," McConaghy continued.

"Why Temagami?" I queried.

"Temagami is where he learned all his skills — trapping, paddling, speaking Ojibwa, falling in love." McConaghy looked distant, sad; I knew he had lost his family in a car accident many years ago. He quickly turned from the subject of love. "But he was a character, too — he loved to play jokes, get into trouble a lot. He hated authority." McConaghy looked at me and winked. I knew what he was thinking, and I knew why he was so set on selling Temagami to me.

I read the book; and then I read it again, slowly, processing each word, all the while looking at the map of Temagami, and of northern Ontario and Quebec. Abitibi country, Biscotasing, Mississaga River — the Land of Shadows beyond the rail, and beyond civilization.

When I first ventured to Temagami in the early spring of 1970, paddling solo in a fourteen-foot cedar-canvas canoe, with the snow falling and the ice still partially on the lake, I passed through a portal into another world — Grey Owl's world — and I knew I had found my home. Having read all of Grey Owl's books, I was primed to discover the very places he paddled and lived, to meet the people who taught him his skills, and perhaps live as he did in the Canadian hinterland.

Bear Island, reserve home of the Teme-Augama Anishnabai, was just as I had imagined. Pulling my canoe up on the beach beside the big dock,

I looked up the wooden plankway to the Hudson's Bay Company store and imagined nothing had changed since Grey Owl's days, sixty years before. I envisioned him sitting on the front steps, jawing with the locals, possibly re-provisioning for a trip up to the trout streams. Not yet the Canadian icon, author, and conservationist, or even Grey Owl — he was just Archie Belaney, lost soul looking for a niche to fit into … just like me.

Most of my adult life has been a compendium of incidental experiences, usually involving something to do with canoeing or the outdoors. I had gained some exposure after my first book was published — a guide to Temagami canoe routes — and a reputation as a canoe ranger in Temagami. I suppose, for some reason, my peers had contrasted my life against that of the renowned Indian imposter, inferring that I was the "modern Grey Owl." Laughing off any assertions that I was *just like him*, I refuted any possibility that I could be anything close to this scallywag. In many ways, that's exactly what he was. There were enough negative traits about Grey Owl that any similarities between him and me could be ill-defined … until I thought about it.

Eight years ago I received a phone call from an Ojibwa elder from Temagami, Alex Mathias, whom I had met briefly at the Temagami environmental roadblock in 1989, but had had no contact with since. He told me that we had to meet, that he had something to tell me concerning a series of dreams he recently had. Alex was revered as a "practising shaman" — an elder who had moved off the reserve at Bear Island to live on his own family hunting grounds on Obabika Lake; to the Anishnabai, dreams were an intrinsic indicator of important events or purpose.

I met him at the Warrior Games, and he insisted that we paddle in the races together. The reason why this sudden, impulsive friendship was materializing, Alex informed me, was the fact that his dreams had revealed that I was his warrior brother; that I was born into the white world by mistake, and that in past lives we hunted and fought together. He said my name was *mahingan webedah* — "wolf-tooth."

When a virtual stranger tells you that he's your warrior brother, and that your name is Wolf-Tooth, you can't help feel a bit overwhelmed. And how does one question this abrupt revelation; it was like finding out you were adopted and your parents weren't really your birth parents. The more I thought about it, the more I believed that this could have been the reason why I had gravitated to the Indian world when I was young, and into my adulthood. Even my art showed an aboriginal influence.

I could see how a young Archie Belaney could believe that he had been born into the white world by accident; and, by impulsive intuition, eventually grow into the world he had every right to be in. Perhaps it was all a masquerade, a ruse, an act to gain recognition for a cause, maybe to assuage a blossoming ego, or maybe something deeper that nobody, even Archie Belaney himself, could possibly understand. Maybe there is something to this afterlife business.

I reflected on my own life, the similarities to Grey Owl that might parallel our lives and I was astonished at what I found. My parents were dysfunctional; I was enthralled by the natural world and Indian life when I was young; I went to Temagami when I was nineteen, same age as Archie; had become a canoe ranger and guide for the same amount of time as Archie; was a crusader for the wilderness on a local and global scale; had authored several books about the wilderness and, on the obstinate wilder side, could never adjust to marriage, abhorred the loss of personal freedom, and could never assimilate to civil life.

But Archie Grey Owl was never my hero. I admired his pithy form of writing and I was smitten wholeheartedly by the lifestyle he lived and by the places he'd been. He was an interesting man with many flaws and shortcomings: a womanizer with shades of chauvinistic maladjustments; an egoist with a sometimes narrow-minded tolerance for other nationalities (prone to generalizations and typecasting); prone to heavy drinking, bouts of depression, and uncontrollable fits of anger. I couldn't possibly be like that, could I? I had never fought in a war and been shot in the foot, but I was on the front lines of the enviro movement, in life-threatening activities, and I had certainly shot myself in the foot several times over the years. It turned out I was more like him than not. The similarities were blazoned on our records, clear as a mountain stream, incontrovertible evidence.

But the question arises: What if he were alive today, what would he be like, and how would he fit in? I thought if I could think like him, having lived somewhat of an analogous life, I could write him into my stories; after all, he had haunted my footsteps for years and his name was synonymous with Temagami, and Temagami was my life and my home. It was ludicrous to think that we would be compatible as canoe mates, or even friends, although he could be that annoying voice of reprove over the shoulder whenever I screwed up. Archie Grey Owl could be the *genius tutelae*, an invisible (except to me) ministering angel — or the devil in deerskins as succinctly coined by Anahareo, his young lover. Perhaps, today, he would be the "devil in polypropylene" — a wannabe Survivorman, or Mantracker.

The stories in this book are real ... with a slight twist. For those who are not familiar with the story of Grey Owl, or of his writings, the juxtaposition of the historic character within my own writings may seem peculiar. If this were the case, it may encourage the reader to investigate the strange story of Archie Belaney, Canada's first wilderness advocate and wildlife conservationist. There have been many biographies written about Grey Owl, written more as an assessment of his actions, as a psychologist pries a client for honest convictions; yet, for me, having walked many of the same paths as Owl, the psychology behind his actions is easily traced, compared, and analyzed in my own meanderings. I know what it is like to succumb to the call of the wilderness trail beyond all measure of logic in a world pulling apart at the seams, and the anguish of unrequited love for which there is no cure but for the companionship of hard drink. For the Grey Owl aficionado, these ramblings may help to reveal or illustrate, or even justify, the rationale behind Archie's troubled soul.

PART ONE

STORIES FROM THE EDGE OF THE WORLD

In the context of drawing similarities between two rebellious individuals who preferred the company of wild animals to people, the *world* in this section eludes to any place outside the familiar realm of understanding and not necessarily of a global, geographical import. To Grey Owl, despite his far-flung popularity, the world revolved around his associations with a rather small part of the Canadian landscape. To all intents and purposes, Grey Owl lived on the edge of the "civilized" world, beyond what he calls the "road" or "rail." It was the avariciousness of a changing world that influenced him greatly, from the mismanagement of natural resources, a growing consumerist mentality, war, and economic depression, Owl crammed several lifetime's into one. Although not a world traveller, he had the vision of an oracle as it pertained to the environmental movement from a global perspective.

1

WHAT THE FOQUE?

Recipe for Baby Seal Stew

One fresh-clubbed "beater"
Boil meat for 1.5 hours
Bouillon: 4 apples, 1 onion, *feuilles de Laurier*, salt and
  pepper
Save juice and meat only

Brown sauce: add
  1 quarter cup butter
  3 cups oil
  3 cups *soupe faire* (thickening)
  bovril
  Carrots, celery, turnips, onions, potatoes
  (1 hour after meat is in)

Mix together 15 minutes then cover meat with vegetables
and cook for 3 hours at 325 degrees Fahrenheit. Serve
topped with poutine. Optional: *croquet signole* (puffin)
cooked in seal fat.

I picked up the phone in my room.

"You gotta get outta there now! Your cover's blown … they're throwing everybody off the island!"

It was Stephen Hurlbut, news director for Citytv in Toronto. His voice was frantic.

"Hunter and Southgate have their tape. They've taken refuge in the hospital. You can't go out on the ice floes tomorrow … we've been trying to get a hold of you for three hours …" The line crackled and went dead.

Shit, now what?

There were voices in the hallway, shouts, obscenities in Québécois and broken English, banging on all the doors. Someone was dragging an empty black body bag behind them.

"Ou est dat focking Paul Watson … where is dat seal-loving piece of sheeit?"

I started packing up my things and camping gear in my backpack but I didn't leave the Auberge Madeli Inn, not just then anyway — there was no place to go. Paul Watson's room was upstairs, directly over my room.

There were at least thirty angry sealers, or *sealbillies* as Paul Watson called them, gathered outside Watson's hotel room. One man began smashing the door with the back of an axe, another with an ice pick, others with beefy fists, but the thick door held firm against the constant blows. Inside sat two Québécois police officers, both wearing sealskin boots; across from them, sitting on the edge of the bed, was environmentalist Paul Watson.

This is it, thought Watson. *I'm going to die right here.*

Watson looked to the cops.

"Are you going to stop them?" Watson asked. The two cops looked at each other and shrugged their shoulders as if they didn't understand the question.

"If they [sealers] get out of hand, we can't help you," the police had told Watson's entourage, which included actor and activist Martin Sheen, and the media.

The door finally splintered open and the mob pushed to get inside at Watson. The cops stepped aside and let them in. Watson was now backed against the wall, inside a semi-circle of sealbillies who wanted nothing less than Watson's skinned hide hanging on the wall of the Seal Hunter's Association office in Cap-aux-Meules. Langford, the beefiest of the sealers, stepped forward and smashed Watson in the side of the face with his fist. Watson flew back against the window, breaking the glass and pulling down the curtains. Watson reached in his pocket for his stun gun and pointed it at Langford before he could deliver the next blow — a powerful punch that could have killed him. Langford fell back on the floor, dazed. Two other sealers fell to the floor, wondering what the burning sensation was that knocked them down. Just as the wave of men pressed Watson against the wall amidst a barrage of kicks and punches, a dozen cops came in beating the mob off with their nightsticks. One cop spit in Watson's face; Watson returned the sentiment.

Watson was dragged outside into the parking lot, shoved in the back seat of a car, and driven to the airport at Havre-aux-Maisons. A Québécois tactical team was flown to the Magdalen Islands to escort the media and *Sea Shepherd* crew out of the province. Someone threw a brick through the car window and struck Watson in the head. From there he was flown to the mainland, New Brunswick, where he was hospitalized for his injuries. Sealers ransacked his room and stole five thousand dollars from his wallet. Apart from the mob that attacked Watson there were over 250 sealers congregated at the hotel, accosting reporters and media delegates, demanding their video tapes, and smashing cameras. The cops were now a part of the mob. A BBC journalist was beaten up and his camera stolen. Environmentalists and media took refuge in their rooms, some blockading their doors with whatever they could pile against them, while others made an escape into the cold night by jumping from their second-floor windows.

Bob Hunter was covering the story for Citytv, along with his cameraman, Todd Southgate, and they had escaped to the hospital across the road from the inn. Bob took the cassette tape from the camera and gave it to another reporter to smuggle back to Toronto. Todd would have died before letting his camera go. By morning light there were only two of us left at the Auberge; me and a reporter from London who was flying home in a couple of hours. I had decided to stay on the island, but it wasn't safe for me to stay at the hotel, or in the village; the only thing to do was to find a place to pitch my tent and hide out for a few days.

Explorer Jacques Cartier visited Îles-de-la-Madeleine, better known as the Magdalen Islands, in 1534; however, the Mi'kmaq had been harvesting walruses there for hundreds of years. The tiny islands form a small archipelago in the Gulf of St. Lawrence, closer to Prince Edward Island but under the jurisdiction of the Province of Quebec. Since 1755, the islands have been inhabited mostly by the French, many of whom are direct descendants of the early Acadians, and from the survivors of the four hundred or more shipwrecks around the archipelago. Until the twentieth century, the islands were completely isolated during the winter, since the pack ice made any trips to the mainland impossible. The winter of 1910 was particularly difficult, and with no way to communicate their peril, letters were written and put inside an empty molasses barrel, or puncheon, and set adrift. It landed shortly after on the shore of Cape Breton, whereupon learning of the Madelinots desperate needs, the government sent an icebreaker with supplies to the islands.

There is no doubt that Magdalen folk are a hardy bunch. Some of Quebec's oldest English-speaking settlements are located here at Old Harry and Entry Island, now assimilated into the francophone population. Census shows a declining population hovering at just over thirteen thousand, probably because the fishing industry has taken a nosedive from over-harvesting — just like the walrus, once plentiful around the islands, but quickly exterminated by over-hunting by the end of the eighteenth century. The mainstay occupations today are lobster fishing and tourism. In the summer it is the miles of white sand beaches and eroding sandstone cliffs that attract the curious; but it's the late-winter eco-tourists who flock to the island to observe the birthing of harp seal pups who have the island buzzing. Camera-toting Germans and Asians trip over each to get a look at one of the cutest creatures on the planet. All they have to do is climb aboard an island commercial helicopter and get dropped off on the nearby ice floes for an hour. What the tourists didn't know was that the helicopter pilot was informing seal hunters on the shore of the locations of clusters of seals. Sealbillies would move in once the eco-tourists were comfortably ensconced in their hotel rooms.

In 1994, the Canadian government began to provide subsidies to reopen the seal hunt, and then financed research into new markets: the Shanghai Fisheries of Taiwan contracts to slaughter 60,000 seals for their penises; the following year, Canada reopens full-scale commercial and sport hunting of seals.

In the words of a buyer from Singapore:

> I am confident that this product will be a sales success all over Asia. In China there are over a thousand years of wisdom and tradition in the use of seal organs as an expedient of sexual potency. In earlier times, only the Emperor was allowed to drink this panacea of potency, a mixture concocted from the penises of reindeer, bulls, and seals, together with Chinese herbs and spirits. And indeed, the Emperor would have needed all the help he could get in bed, to fulfill the obligations he had towards his innumerable wives and concubines.

PENIS RESTAURANT OPENS IN BEIJING

One specialty, Canadian seal penis, costs a hefty £220,
and requires ordering in advance.

In early May of 1995 I received a call from Toronto's Citytv news director, Stephen Hurlbut, who called to see if I was interested in doing some undercover environmental work. I had been shooting enviro-documentaries with City's ecologist specialist, Bob Hunter, co-founder of Greenpeace, and was eager to work with Bob on a new venture. The difference here, though, was that I would be working alone this time: the plan was to infiltrate a group of seal hunters on the Magdalen Islands and get candid video of them clubbing baby seals.

Because I had a valid gun licence I could escapade as a visiting tour consultant, scoping out future seal hunts for wealthy sport hunters. A bow hunter had already booked an April hunt to bag a trophy harp seal with the locals. It was a fresh market for the Seal Hunters' Association and the tourism department. Magdalen officials had effectively kept the press and public out of range of the hunt by legislating strict "observer-only" permits, unless you had a bona fide licence to kill, then you could find yourself a sponsor who would validate a hunting licence for killing seal for sport. The sponsor had to be an island hunter, or a member of the seal "crew," and I had found my sponsor in short order after a few phone calls to the S.H.A.

Once we arrived at the Quebec City airport for a transfer to a Magdalen flight, Hunter's crew and I remained aloof. There were obvious Islanders waiting to board the same flight, and Hunter stood out like a Magdalen Island lighthouse. Suspicious eyes were cast toward the Citytv crew as if something was up … and there certainly was.

Paul Watson, good friend to Hunter and also a co-founder of Greenpeace (asked to leave the organization because of his hyper-activist slant) was headed to the Magdalen Islands with actor/activist Martin Sheen and entourage. Watson had formed the successful Sea Shepherd Society based out of Los Angeles, and was planning on introducing an alternative to killing seals to hunters by suggesting they comb the shedding hair of the animals and collect it for use in bedding products. Clubbing seals was a two-century-old tradition on the island; to think the men were about to drop their ice picks and clubs and start wielding fur combs some would think a serious misjudgement by Watson … or maybe not. Watson was of the ilk that the combing antic (although a successful practice today) would validate his presence on the island. He was also a scrapper.

In 1977, Watson had brought Brigitte Bardot to visit the seal hunt in the Gulf of St. Lawrence. He locked himself to the winch line of a sealing ship and was subsequently dragged over the ice, in and out of the water, and through a gauntlet of angry sealers on the deck of the boat, all the while being punched and kicked almost senseless. Two years later he was on the ice floes spraying pups with red dye, making the pelts unmarketable. Watson made international press and put a huge dent in the business of selling pelts. But Madelinots don't forget that easily, and in March '94, as Watson steered his group to the islands, preparations were already underway to organize a protest.

I booked in to the Auberge Madeli Inn, main floor, and walked down to the Sealer's Association office. After a few pointed questions, I was hooked up with a local family in the village and invited over that evening to meet with them. I was a bit nervous because not only was I *not* a hunter, but I didn't know much about guns and knew I'd have to bullshit my way through any conversation on the subject. It was a young couple; his family came from a long line of seal clubbers and he was happy to walk me through the pages of a scrap book filled with photographs of dead animals. He asked far too many questions,

"So, what rifle do they shoot de bear wit in Ontario, eh?"

"30:30 … or even a .22 sometimes if you're good at it," I answered. The young hunter looked a bit stunned.

"30:30, huh?" He paused. "I would've thought mehbe a .247 or .217 good fer dat." An uneasy silence. He went on to talk about bullets. What the fuck did I know about bullets? He told me he couldn't kill the white pups anymore, just the four-week-old "beaters," as they were called, when the fur was starting to turn black.

"Audette Leblanc makes nice sealskin hats and coats." He suggested I purchase some souvenirs after our rendezvous with his crew, two days later. We were to meet just off Cap du Dauphin on the East Island and they said I could bring my camera. I was in … at least for the next twenty-four hours, until Paul Watson arrived.

There was a poster of actor Martin Sheen hanging in a video shop window in town when I had arrived. When the proprietor heard that Sheen was part of Watson's entourage, the poster was quickly removed and replaced with one advertising a French flick. There was a pall through the village of Cap-aux-Meules but the inn was abuzz with reporters and international journalists getting rooted for some kind of showdown. I sat at the bar alone and eyed Bob Hunter sitting with Southgate, the videographer, in a far corner. There were a few local men at the bar, drinking slowly, listening and not talking at all. Not a good sign. They were probably "keeping an eye on things" at the hotel, waiting for Watson to arrive.

Hunter brushed by me — a sign to meet in the men's washroom. Standing at the urinals, we exchanged information and thoughts. I told him I was going out on the floes in a couple of days.

"*Sheeit*, that might be bad news," Bob said. I asked him why.

"Watson's on his way here now and the locals are looking for blood."

"What, here to the hotel?" I questioned, thinking that he wasn't staying at this hotel and not coming until the next day.

"Watch your back, that's all … it's not worth getting killed over," Bob warned. I went back to the bar after Bob had left. Watson showed up soon after with a couple of his crew off the boat. I'd already met Watson and he knew not to say anything to me. He went right over to Bob and Todd and sat down. The local men at the bar left. Watson was on a high; he and one of his mates had the inn open up the adjoining bowling lanes and they started tossing balls. I didn't like the feeling of being this close to Watson or Hunter in case the locals thought I was in any way connected. I left the bar and noticed Sheen and a handful of police talking in the lobby. Sheen looked frightened and was talking rapidly, and waving his arms, trying to be understood. Pickup trucks were filing into the inn parking lot. I went to my room and phoned my local seal hunter contact but got no answer. I slept uneasily.

Two hours later I woke up to men shouting in the halls. I went for a walkabout but the hotel lobby was packed with sealbillies and cops, spilling out down the halls with loose bands of sealers breaking off from the crowd to look for Watson. Things went from bad to worse. There was no way I was going out on any ice floe with four incensed sealbillies.

The snow was blowing so hard, pelting the small tent with such a force that I thought I was going to be lifted off the ground completely. Even the shelter of the spruce seemed sparse protection from the Atlantic gale that swept across the islands. I had driven the rented car as far as I could: somewhere between Havre Aubert and L'Étang-des-Caps I found a short laneway off the main road and parked, grabbed my pack, and hiked into the hills. The TV station had booked us rooms at the inn but I didn't trust the situation I had put myself in and had brought along my camping gear just in case. It was crazy for me to stay in the village, as my intentions to get film from a hunt were conspicuously devious. It was nearly dark when I had trekked into the thickest part of the Magdalen Islands — an inhospitable, rugged wilderness core about five kilometres across. The resident snow was crusted from thawing and freezing and I had walked about a kilometre over several hummocks and found some security in a copse of spruce trees, pitched my tent, and settled in for the night.

I wrote in my journal by candlelight. The two candles exuded just enough ambient heat to keep frost from forming in the tent and maintain a temperature just above freezing. I mused about a Grey Owl story I had read years before, about a time when he was caught in a blizzard and suffering from snowblindness and had to make an emergency camp. I had learned some of my skills from his mistakes, such as making snow goggles from birchbark, cutting slits for eye-holes, and wearing them while on long winter treks across open lakes in bright sunshine. And, to always have survival gear with you, no matter what the occasion; in the least, waterproof matches, a ground tarp, and warm clothes. I wondered what Archie would do in this situation …

"*You got yourself in a real fix now, eh, shaganash?*" Owl said.

"*Shit, Archie, what are you doing here?*" I said to the man materializing across from me, hunched in the far corner of the tent, barely visible in the candlelight. It was creepy.

"*The only thing missing here, shaganash, is a bottle of Dewar's,*" Owl bewailed.

"*Since when did you start drinking on the trail?*" I noticed he was wearing a sealskin coat. I questioned Owl about it. "*And the coat … what's with the coat, Archie? Are you supporting these sealbillies?*"

"*Well, it's no different with trapping beaver. It's a tradition with the sealers. It's more sport than economics. There's little money in it anymore but it's all about lifestyle and their rights,*" Owl said.

"*But the brutality of it … the pups, the media?*" I was pleading now.

"*I know about the brutality of clubbing young beaver to death, listening to their screams and death moans. My heart turned to stone. I shut it out …*

until Gertie came into my life. For me it was the money, survival, I didn't know what else to do."

"But the sealers, Archie, they don't need the money — they're lobster fishermen. Look at this place, the villages, the new homes ... there are two new trucks in every driveway, malls, a Tim Hortons in Cap-aux-Meules. I didn't see one impoverished shack anywhere on the Magdalens."

Archie smiled. *"You know the answer, shaganash, it's staring you in the face. Just like the loggers in Temagami. These people have a harsh life. They work hard for what they have, and they resent outsiders telling them what to do in their own backyard. They blame the seals for the lack of fish. They care nothing about the science or morality of it all, just like the government cares nothing about conservation ... until it's too late already. Are you sure you don't have any Dewar's?"*

Archie faded into the flapping tent fabric, his thin voice trailing off until all I could hear was the wailing of the wind outside.

I had acquired two bits of information before Watson arrived and spoiled everything. The helicopter company said they were flying in teams of German eco-tourists that same week; my young sealbilly contact also eluded to the fact that the helicopter pilots often radioed to onshore seal hunters the location of seals out on the floes. Overeager tourists were unconsciously supporting the seal hunt, waving cameras in front of birthing seals, traumatizing the mothers, followed by local hunters wielding guns, clubs, and gaff-hooks.

I stood on the snow-covered Dune de l'Ouest, off Havre aux Basques, using an old shipwrecked tanker as cover and photographing seal hunters pushing their "banana" boats out into the Gulf, working their way out toward where the helicopters had just returned from the ice floes.

At the time, in 1975, seal meat was worth thirty-five cents a pound; the market price for the pelt was ten dollars, and a seal penis went for fifteen dollars. Two years later, the value of a seal penis escalated to as much as seventy dollars. In 1998, the price of a seal penis dropped back to fifteen dollars because of the availability of Viagra in China and Japan. The market price for combed seal hair was three hundred dollars per pound.

In May of 2008, Paul Watson received a package delivered directly to his door. Inside was a T-shirt emblazoned with the words PHOQUE

YOU PAUL WATSON, a caricature of him, and a fist with middle finger extended. There was also a letter signed by 2,321 Madelinots bearing the same words. Watson graciously thanked them for the gift:

> That was very thoughtful, and all you knuckle-dragging, baby seal serial killers from the Magaderthal Isles — a very appreciative *merci beaucoup*. From what I hear, the sealers think that this is a pretty wonderful play on words. As one sealer told *Canadian Press*, "ya know da French word for seal is 'phoque,' so we are saying 'phoque you Paul Watson' … get it?"
>
> Translated literally, it means "Seal You Paul Watson." As for what they mean it to say, well, quite frankly, I'm flattered. Getting 2,321 sealbillies to take the time to send a collective "phoque you" on paper took initiative, and it took time, and I can only assume they had the time and they were able to sign because we chased them off the ice floes.
>
> With the clubs silenced, they took up silk-screening instead.

It felt good to be flying back home. The plane was almost empty. The media had scattered and retreated, and Paul Watson was licking his wounds. Watson had called the Madelinots "cowards" for what they did to him, but for the gulf fishermen, who face dangers from living off an oftentimes vicious sea, the derogatory label certainly does not apply. The seal is not an endangered animal, and the Madelinots take only about two thousand out of a population of several hundred thousand.

On such sensitive animal-rights issues there are always additional considerations, particularly when aboriginal or even simply cultural traditions come in to play. Activists often direct their anger against the wrong party. Participants in the fashion markets that control the fur industry, or any animal-part commerce, tend to be ignorant of the plight of the creatures involved, or just don't care. On the subject of tolerance,

Grey Owl states that, "much of the cruelty perpetrated to provide fashion adornment is not realized, or even suspected, by the wearers who, somewhat unjustly, get most of the blame." True to an extent, but from the perspective of an environmental strategist, though, it is paramount to first educate the public, and this sometimes requires drastic measures. In the case of the Magdalen seal hunters, I found that the animal, for the most part, is wisely used, but I am not in favour of fur for fashion and believe the fight should be directed at those who drive the market for such things.

The afternoon was cloudless, and we flew at about ten thousand feet heading back across the Gaspé Peninsula to Quebec City. Below was a checkerboard of clearcuts and roads, clearly visible as white, snow-blanketed swaths and ribbony veins with no discernable natural pattern left to the landscape. Green tufts of forest stood out like blistered sores: Wilderness gone.

I remembered that Archie and Anahareo escaped to the vicinity of Lac Temiscouata, Quebec, in the mid 1920s, looking for a place to set up a beaver colony. Checking my map, I could see the lake below and the town of Cabano on its west shore, the village where Archie collected his mail — the fifteen dollars a month army disability pension cheque — and mailed off his first article, "The Falls of Silence," to *Country Life Magazine* in England.

It was hard to distinguish where they had trekked in to build their cabin — somewhere up the Touladi River toward the New Brunswick border. Archie wrote about the already wasted landscape on the arduous trip into Birch Lake, and his disillusionment at the loss of wilderness and possible scarcity of game. The desecration of wildlife habitat, the construction of invasive roads, transfigured the natural environment to one of hackneyed uselessness. Tree stands were now an anomaly on the landscape. Archie was lucky that he made his own transformation here quickly, from bemused animal rehabilitator, ex-trapper, to writer and entertainer. It was the beginning of a new career for Grey Owl, but the end of a love relationship for Archie Belaney.

As for the seals and the mentality behind the hunt, Belaney well knew the Law of the North and the sometimes merciless killings perpetrated for a meagre livelihood. The arrogance of the slaughter, whether it be beaver or baby seals, rests on the merits of tradition and what northerners feel is their God-given right, their inherited property, and their manly primitive pleasures.

GREY OWL CHEESE

Made at Fromagerie Le Detour in Notre-Dame-du-Lac,
Quebec
By Ginette Begin and Mario Quirion.
It refers to the colour but also in honour of
Archie Belaney who
lived for some time near Lac Temiscouata,
influencing the region
near the cheese factory

2

GARBAGE RANGER

*The Wilderness should now no longer be considered as a
playground for vandals, or a rich treasure trove to be ruth-
lessly exploited for the personal gain of the few — to be
grabbed off by whoever happens to get there first.*
— Grey Owl, *Tales of an Empty Cabin*, Preface

One of the benefits of growing up in the country is the certainty that
there is a country dump nearby. As a kid, like any country kid would
do on a Saturday afternoon, I would ride my bike to the dump. I wasn't
like some other kids who went there with pellet rifles to shoot rats or
abandoned cats; I was more interested in *stuff* — any gadgets, trinkets,
or miscellany that looked old or interesting, and which would fit comfortably in my backpack or could be strapped on to my bike carrier and
whisked home. These treasures would sometimes adorn whatever fort I
was building, used as a mock gun or sword, or just horded and buried
amongst other stuff that was piled on the floor of my clothes closet. One
man's garbage is another boy's treasure.

I was, and still am, a dedicated, dyed-in-the-wool packrat. I buy my
clothes at Sally Ann and Goodwill, for no other reason except I like old
stuff, and it's unfashionably comfortable because someone else has already
broken it in. I have an insatiable appetite for garage sales, flea markets,
and estate auctions. And what people will throw away, at any given time,

usually trademarks a particular period in their lives and explains the state of affairs in the world around them. Garbage is a very personal thing; it identifies our life habits and archives our accomplishments and defeats. As a species we produce more garbage and waste than we know what to do with. It's a consumerist society conundrum, and as such, we cast our detritus without remorse, without pity, and without sentimentality.

Archie and I paddled into a small bay, about halfway up the north arm of Lake Temagami, and beached the canoe at a well-used campsite. He hated sitting in the bow, not so much that he needed to be in control of the canoe, but that his constant barrage of comments would be lost in the wind. He grumbled as he passed me, garbage bag in hand, and sauntered off along a trail behind the tent sites.

"*It's just tin, dammit,*" Archie said with a look of total disgust on his face. He knew where to go.

"*Yeah, but it's your garbage ... shore lunches, remember, when you guided at Camp Keewaydin. When you couldn't catch fish and you fed the clients corned beef out of tins.*"

My remarks went unnoticed. He came back ten minutes later and dropped a half-filled sac at my feet, danced a sort of Irish-cum-war-dance-jig around me, and let out a loud whoop.

"*Feel better now, Owl?*" I asked.

"*Yes, absolved I am, sir, of my abhorrent camping skills ... a better man for it, too, I might add,*" Archie answered without a lick of sincerity.

From 1977 to 1984 I was a garbage ranger. I much preferred the title of park or canoe ranger, or even resource technician II as prescribed by my job application form, but the cognomen of *garbage ranger* was coined by the regional director — a fickle man who spent his career wholesaling Ontario forests to logging companies. Brushing out canoe portages and cleaning garbage from campsites as a part of the government responsibility mandate didn't quite fit into his narrow-minded rationale. My job to keep canoe route portage trails clear of deadfall and brush eventually expanded into a major garbage cleanup of gargantuan proportion, and at the time, the wilderness was one huge dumping ground for just about everything. Trash was dumped with impunity, everywhere, and by everyone, scattered about the green earth with a pronounced glee, unchecked, sometimes resourcefully concealed under stumps and rocks, half-buried, or just left in garbage bags as if by the curb for weekly pickup, only to be picked apart by bear, skunk, and raven.

Temagami was a vast wilderness at one time, and had not yet yielded to the lumberman's axe, and for nearly half a century, up until the Second World War, was paradise for the sportsman, canoeist, and purveyor of adventure. On Lake Temagami, the rustic log lodges were full, guides (like Archie Belaney) were busy, and kids from southern prep schools flocked to summer camps. And all their garbage had to go somewhere … and years later it became my job to clean it all up.

Out of sight, out of mind … the old adage about not caring about something you did wrong so long as you can't see it — like idling your SUV in a parking lot with the air conditioner on or waiting in line for your take-out coffee, doing your part for climate change.

When people discard their waste, there is no measure of deviant ways in which they do it — that is, when conventional garbage pickup is not an option. Smokers flick their still-lit butts out their car windows (often causing wildfires), or discretely empty their ashtrays in parking lots or curbside, then drive off with a sense of godliness. Cottagers once bagged their weekly garbage, packed it in their motor launches, and dumped it overboard into the lake. This was not a clandestine approach to waste management — it was more of a social excursion where cottagers could exchange morning salutations and afternoon invitations for drinks on their respective docks.

Dumping waste into our streams, lakes, and rivers is something we Canadians do well, and we've been at it since white Europeans landed on our shores four centuries ago. Prior to this there was no such thing as garbage in Canada. Aboriginal Canadians had no use for it. Fecal waste and animal leftovers were eaten by the ravens and other woodland creatures, and when things started to smell bad, the residents simply moved their village a hundred metres down the shoreline. Since everything was organic, Nature dealt with it accordingly, neatly and efficiently. When whites started building their interior forts, usually on major trade rivers, all the winter garbage was piled on to the ice and allowed to flush away during the spring melt. That at least got rid of half their garbage problem; the rest was disposed of in the infamous "can dump" usually located not far behind the living quarters.

As a ranger, given the task to "clean up the wilderness" gave me great insight into the complexities of human nature when it comes to the deposition (and disposition) of garbage. There were many perpetrators. But back in the "old" days, it wasn't a moral or ethical (and certainly not an ecological) consideration; it was simply a matter of fact that you disposed of your trash in any way so long as you couldn't see it. A can dump was established at all campsites and behind lodges and cottages, but because most cottages and lodges on Lake Temagami were on islands, owners were loathe to have a can dump desecrate their private space. So the customary can dump was established nearby on the mainland, just far enough back so those nimrods trolling for shoreline walleye couldn't eye it.

Those righteous canoeheads who beam with self-adulation about "no-trace camping," and those guiltless, tree-hugging, granola-munching "enviro-mentalists" had their roots buried deep in trash. It was code for paddlers to burn and flatten their tin cans and to dispose of them in the campsite can dump. And after half a century, the can dumps flourished into heaped mounds of refuse. With the advent of plastic, modern campers simply added to the can dumps with stuff that took millennia to biodegrade. The layers of plastic garbage, though, added a protective shield over the old tins of bully-beef, so when my crew and I descended on them for removal, some of the century-old tin cans looked as if they had been tossed a week ago; labels, still intact, denoted the era in which the contents were consumed. The can dump was the perfect way to sift through the layers of Canadian history.

The Ontario government had no interest in dealing with all the wilderness garbage; in fact, it was common practice for our provincial stewards of nature, up until the 1980s, to establish yet more garbage dumps within parks and heavily used recreation areas. This in itself added greatly to the physical problem of mounting refuse, *and* sent out a clear message to the sloppy camper that it was okay to toss your garbage in the bush and not to pack it out. In Temagami, where the soils are thin at best, or just bedrock, a dump quickly became an overflowing cesspit. When the garbage began spilling out over the countryside, and the purists complained about the desecration of paradise, the bureaucrats sent me in to tidy things up.

To clean up a sizeable dump that had blossomed for several years, and in the middle of wilderness where there are no roads, the job became a technical nightmare. Tin cans had to be flattened with the back of an axe — cans half-filled with a fetid mixture of dead mice, maggots, and other slimy matter that would splatter up in your face as you pounded away; bottles were broken down so the shards would fit into the larger tin cans for safe export. All had to be neatly compacted and bagged carefully to be flown out in the government Beaver aircraft. Garbage was often transported by canoe for several miles to a pickup point where the plane could land.

Fishermen were the worst offenders. Wherever they could fly in or access campsites by boat, the trash heap was impressive. Aside from dousing several "shore-lunch" wildfires, it was always a leather-glove affair with clean-up duty, often having to extricate homespun toilets made out of five-gallon pails filled to the brim with the greasy by-products of tinned chili and cheap wine. On one occasion, having landed the patrol boat at a well-used campsite after a couple of balmy summer weeks of use by fishermen, we went about our task of cleaning up the sordid mess. There being certain recondite skills a park ranger must possess, tolerance and ingenuity being prime tenets of good stewardship practices, there are also times the romance of trail life wears thin as sausage skins and the job loses its glamour.

Shit, when packed in a plastic bag and hung in a densely branched spruce tree and left to ferment for a couple of weeks in summer weather, expands like a balloon, stretched tight until near bursting point. Because I came across this particular bit of garbage it was deemed my responsibility to de-snag it and dispose of it while the rest of my crew looked on with bated amusement. It was like trying to defuse a bomb and snipping the right wire to disarm it. After working the taut bag of excrement through the worst of the snags I was just about clear when a pungy-stick appeared out of nowhere. I fumbled; the bag tilted toward the sharp point and abruptly exploded in my hands, a fecal shower covering me from head to foot while my crewmates cajoled and ran for the lake — with me in hot pursuit. I cursed those fishermen and wished them all a heinous demise.

As budgets ran thin for backcountry maintenance and money poured into timber harvesting and road building, I could no longer conscript the services of the government plane to fly garbage out of the park systems. Instead, I had to start burying garbage discreetly in excavated pits (as instructed by my supervisor) in bedrock-thin soils that were only inches deep. Sometimes there was up to fifty bags of collected garbage sitting in our canoes, and we searched high and low for earth deep enough to bury the trash. There was no easy solution but we did manage to dispose of it neatly but not without much physical labour, nor shortage of verbal assaults against the bureaucracy.

In the great beyond, past the point of easy access by boat or road, along the wilderness trail travelled only by ardent adventurers, there exists a plethora of dirty little secrets. There are those who have expended their tolerance for the ardour of the trail; packs too heavy with gear and food, energy spent on the steep portage climbs, the incessant scourge of biting insects, the longing for home and easy life. Stuff gets left on the trail. Good stuff: axes, propane stoves, expensive clothing, anything to lighten the load before the long carry. And the garbage so neatly bagged that suddenly becomes too heavy to pack out finds its way under a stump or rock at the head of a portage trail. I know. I'm an expert at finding garbage. The soiled underwear, the spent condoms, the sanitary napkin, disposable diapers — the effluent of daily industry, tucked not-so-discreetly out of sight, quickly and self-assumingly, justifiably to lighten the load and the stress of travail, covered scantily in sphagnum moss or lichen-crusted rock, hopefully obscure from the passerby. But it never really is. I know where to look; usually a bear sniffing around has dislodged it, or dragged it off, but tired of its unpalatableness and left it in full view anyway. That is the way with the modern wilderness. And today, years after my shift as garbage ranger, there is always the guilt as I portage along a trail and step over that tidbit of garbage and make no attempt to pick it up, the memory of packing out over three thousand bags of garbage still resounding distastefully loud between my ears.

The most satisfying aspect of my job was to set up a "garbage" sting operation. Having just cleaned up a campsite of all refuse, to the point where you could eat off the rocks, my crew and I would retire close by, but out of sight, and wait for a canoe group or fishing party to set up their camp on the freshly sanitized campsite. Short of carrying a sidearm (a request that was turned down by my supervisor), we were armed only with a two-way radio on which, due to the rugged topography and distance from the forestry office, communication was unreliable. The following morning, after the party had packed up and left, we would scoot in and check the campsite for any refuse left behind. If it was substantial, then we would race to catch the group and return the garbage to them with a stern warning. One such party, having just vacated the site and heading down the lake, saw us paddling toward them; recognizing the government emblem on the side of the canoe, they began to paddle faster. A race soon unfolded and it turned out that they were proficient canoeists and it was much work to keep up. After thirty-five kilometres in rough water, we finally caught up to them, presented them with their half-bag of garbage while chastising their leader for improprieties cast against the wilderness code.

It was often gruelling, often thankless work, made worse by the fact that most charges against garbage perpetrators were never served in court. I have to admit that my crew, under my command, had become somewhat of a vigilante group, seeking out those habitual litterers with fanatical efficiency. The thirst of enduring such work on blistering hot summer days could never be slaked, because even the lake water was too warm to satisfy our cravings.

Once, after two weeks on the garbage trail, we came across a short portage route used almost exclusively by a local fishing lodge. The lodge had a boat cache at the far end of the trail, allowing their patrons to park their camp boats and walk the portage carrying their fishing gear and lunches only. It took most of a full day to clean the two-hundred-metre trail of all the garbage scattered about; but flipping over a rotted stump at the sight of what looked like a scad of trash, I uncovered a secret stash of beer. It had been set deep in a crevasse, sandwiched between sphagnum hummocks, the temperature of which rivalled that of a refrigerator. Because of the sad state of the portage landing and the unrequited appreciation for cleaning up garbage left by callous nimrods, and not being satisfied at all with having only removed the distributor caps from the outboard motors, we felt no remorse for walking away with their case of cold beer.

3

BLOCKADE!

And the tree that had lived so long, stood patiently and waited for the end. The first axe struck. The tree gave no sign, but stood in all its grand composure and nobility to the last — and then swayed a little, and started on its journey to the ground. With a moaning, screaming cry, as its fibres ripped apart and its sweeping superstructure tore downwards through the air, the mighty conifer crashed to earth ...
— Grey Owl, *Tales of an Empty Cabin*, "The Tree"

John and I were on surveillance. Thankfully there was just enough incident moonlight to find our way along the logging road and to sidetrack through the bush around the parked police cruiser. We left the camp amidst the usual campfire frivolity, shared dope and storytelling, using our headlamps along the dark trail from the trailhead to the logging road. The canopy of pine was thick here but the trail had been well-packed from blockaders trekking out at daybreak to chain themselves to Komatsu bulldozers or harass road supervisors and police. Nobody knew we had left. That was part of the protocol.

It was a two-kilometre hike to where they were building the bridge. Just beyond was a collection of dozers and skidders, lined side by each, waiting for their owners who would show up at eight o'clock the next morning, shuttled in by school bus the forty kilometres from the logging

town of Elk Lake. Beyond the mélange of road-building machinery was the cop car, idling, with two officers inside. It was a warm September night and the only reason to be idling the car was to keep the headlights shining on the machinery. Because of previous incidents with blockaders, the cops were getting more aggressive, staging cruisers and men in various locations overnight, or patrolling the road regularly. The machines were now all parked together and not strung out along the road, which made it problematic for activists to lock on to equipment.

We were crawling on our bellies, no more than a hundred feet from the cop car when the cruiser door opened. One of the officers walked directly toward us as if he'd heard something. He stopped at the edge of the road and took a piss, looked around nervously, and climbed back into his car. Music was turned up louder and we could hear laughter. John and I realized we were being over-cautious, so we walked the rest of the way through the tangle of cedar, crossed the Wakimika River, and emerged back out onto the road without worrying about the cops. They were oblivious to the world outside of the glare of their headlight beam.

After walking only about a kilometre, we heard a car approaching from the west gate, headlights coursing through the treetops above our heads. We dove off the road and down an embankment as another cop car flashed by, followed by a pickup truck. We waited until it was clear before climbing back out onto the road. John and I kept to the far edge of the logging road where our footprints weren't noticeable, and kept up a good pace, walking west, looking for another compound where heavy machinery was purported to be stationed. By now the moon was directly overhead and the sky cloudless, and the coolness of the September night was starting to have its effect, leaving a patina of frost over the landscape, in ghostly, luminescent sheets.

The yellow Komatsus were incandescent; giant insects in the weird moonlight. John and I stood at the edge of the clearing near the trees, kept to the shadows, and waited. There was no movement anywhere in the compound, the only sound was our own breathing. It was too quiet here. The cops watching the road and the equipment back at the river wouldn't suspect that any blockaders would get by their cruiser at night without being spotted. They also didn't figure that anyone would walk the eight kilometres to the west gate equipment compound which was now

completely vulnerable. But we weren't there to do any monkey wrench-
ing — it would have been too obvious. We were simply taking inventory.

We shoved potatoes down the exhaust pipes and left.

Early in 1989, a petition containing the names of sixty-five Canadian and
American biologists and botanists from industry, government, museums,
and academe was sent to Premier David Peterson of Ontario. The scientists had joined the recently formed Temagami Wilderness Society
(TWS) in their call to the Ontario government for a moratorium on logging old-growth forests. Temagami owned some of North America's last
significant old-growth red- and white-pine ecosystems that have been
self-replacing for nearly a thousand years. Sentiment was substantiated
by field studies and past research ... scientists studying old-growth in
the United States agreed that the characteristics of an old-growth forest
cannot be recreated by silviculture or any other methods.

But Ontario Premier David Peterson continued to ignore the plea of
Ontarians to stop the logging of ancient pine in Temagami. This despite
the fact that the Ontario Ministry of Natural Resources in Temagami
had secretly sanctioned the Red Squirrel Road to be built through the
pine-rich Lady Evelyn-Smoothwater Wilderness Park in 1984, and the
discovery and subsequent public outcry over an environmental assessment that had been altered in 1986 (the consulting company involved
having removed its name from the document out of embarrassment).
In addition, Temagami had been listed on the Threatened Areas Register
by the Swiss-based International Union for the Conservation of Nature.

Armed with a cellphone, Andy climbed a tree on the lawn of Queen's
Park in downtown Toronto, found a comfortable perch, and for two days
called Premier Peterson every few minutes, tying up his phone line until
persuaded to come down by metro police.

Legendary folk singer Gordon Lightfoot teamed with Murray
McLaughlin, The Cowboy Junkies, Parachute Club, Blue Rodeo, and

author Farley Mowat to raise money for the TWS to take the fight to protect Temagami pine to the next stage — *the blockade!*

The Temagami Wilderness Society — like the activist group Greenpeace, out of Vancouver — or like most quasi-militant enviro groups anywhere, was formed by a handful of leftwing, free-thinking individuals who wore their passions on their sleeves; passion not just for the cause, but for the fight. Brian Back spearheaded the organization. He was the historian for the oldest boys' camp in North America, Camp Keewaydin; and there was Terry, paralegal for a well-known Tri-Town lawyer and long-time activist since the early seventies. Me, I was the ecotourism whip-dog, just starting a new outfitting business after years as a park ranger. I knew the district inside and out, Brian was the media and organizational expert, and Terry was the legal specialist — a formidable team for the fight. Government and industry were unpractised in the arena of environmental brawling; so were we, but we had time on our side. The *browns* did not have the capacity to make quick decisions or garnish public support through the media, and to win the fight we knew we had to control the fifth estate. Posters of desiccated forests, gargantuan trees, and pristine wilderness being destroyed were splashed all over the front pages of national newspapers. Money poured in to TWS coffers; new office space in the city core gave presence to the organization, and people were hired to run one of Canada's premier (and fastest growing) environmental groups (now Earthroots).

Initially, the fight was to protect the wilderness integrity of the Temagami canoe routes. But the momentum picked up when we adopted the west-coast strategy of protecting ancient forests, and Temagami had plenty of that remaining. The Ontario government, who were in the business of selling timber licences, were negligent in acknowledging any old-growth in the province for fear of reducing harvest inventories. Now they were forced into battle with no battle plan except for sheer authoritarian bully tactics. Passive green action only stirred up the bees nest; the only option was to blockade the road being built through the wilderness park.

But this wasn't just a *white* fight of city-bred, granola-munching green freaks and disgruntled canoeists; the local aboriginal band — the Teme-Augama Anishnabai, or "deep water by the shore People" — had a century-old grudge against the Ontario bureaucracy. The six totem family brands, the loon, kingfisher, rattlesnake, beaver, porcupine, and caribou clans[1] all gathered at their traditional campsite at Sharp Rock Inlet at the north end of Lake Temagami where the infamous Red Squirrel Road entered sacred ground. Led by Chief Gary Potts, in 1988 the TAA held vigil on the road for ninety-five days, from June to September, with tribal fires, religious ceremonies, and demonstrations. STOP THE DEATH ROADS; WE ARE OWNERS OF KA DAKI MENAN, NOT THE UNDERTAKERS OF NDAKI MENAN; and ROAD CLOSED BY AUTHORITY TEME-AUGAMA ANISHNABAI, OWNERS FOR 6,000 YEARS were sloganized banners for the media. It took the government off guard and no arrests were made. The following June, the TAA moved their blockade west to another controversial logging road that was bridging two rivers and encroaching upon sacred ancient forests. It was a brief but defiant show of strength that lasted only three days, but there were eleven arrests this time, indicating that the officials were getting their act together and were willing to play rough.

Now primed and ready and strong, with the backing of the media with their "if it bleeds, it leads" mentality, the Temagami Wilderness Society had plans to blockade the Red Squirrel Road at Wakimika Lake, in the heart of big pine country. Logistics were daunting. Wakimika was remote and would require boat shuttles, or floatplane flights to access the blockade camp, which would be set up on the quarter-mile beach on the lake. Road access was out of the question since the police would not allow any traffic destined for the blockade site to pass through. I had set up the blockade campsite with pit privies, a large canvas prospector tent, firewood, and a trail that was cut a half-kilometre to the road right-of-way — the "path of most resistance," where blockaders would gain access to confront loggers, machine operators, and police. Demonstrations would be planned at the Wakimika River Bridge — the first line of confrontation.

Bob Rae was the new leader of the New Democrats and it wasn't difficult to lure him in to support the burgeoning green movement. It was now mid-September and cool weather was imminent. Blockaders began

---

1.   It is interesting to note that two of the family totem emblems, the rattlesnake and the caribou, once indigenous residents of the Temagami area, have been extirpated to other, remoter parts of the province.

arriving at the campsite, setting up tents, and scouting the road. Crazy Andy was stationed as the camp caretaker; the first task given to him was to climb a tall pine to erect an antenna that connected the two-way radio system back to my outfitting base in Temagami, nearly thirty-five kilometres to the east. Since the police could monitor the radio, we devised a code system in Ojibwa — who was coming in to the camp, supplies needed, number of people — information that would now be gibberish to the cops. September 18 was the big media day: Bob Rae was to be flown in to attend the first official day of the blockade; Bob Hunter — enviro-specialist for Citytv was already at the camp and in party mode; and I was flying in with Darcy Henton, environmental reporter for the *Toronto Star*, along with an ace photographer.

Media day was important for getting the right message across about the illegal road and the cutting of old-growth forest. But when our plane landed, the issue was obfuscated by what was going on at the beach campsite. The warm fall weather had prompted many of the blockaders to shed their clothing; would-be green warriors now ran up and down Paradise Beach in the buff, the camp looking more like a naturist gathering than a blockade camp. One fellow waded out to meet our plane as it was too shallow to beach the aircraft. I nearly stepped on his appendage as it rested on the edge of the pontoon while we were unloading gear. It was all too discomfiting, but I could tell the newspaper reporters were enjoying the façade, scratching notes and taking pictures.

This isn't working, I thought. Things began falling apart.

Blockaders had been at work through the night, scattering logs and rocks over the Red Squirrel Road for several kilometres leading up to the bridge. Bridge timbers were hauled to the middle of the road to form a box to hold a dozen people; some locked themselves to bridge timbers, while Brian Back (executive director of the TWS), had himself buried up to his neck in the middle of the road. At dawn there were nearly one hundred people gathered at the bridge waiting for the police to arrive, banners were erected, and everyone managed to keep their clothes on.

A school bus load of beefy loggers and mill workers had arrived the night before, some carrying baseball bats, and had gathered in a group to one side of the blockaders. When the future premier of Ontario, Bob Rae, arrived, he walked directly to the first group of people and thanked them passionately for coming and supporting the cause. The only trouble was the fact that he was addressing the bevy of disgruntled loggers thinking they were environmentalists.

"Bob, over here … those are the bad guys," came a chorus of voices by the bridge. But Rae was in the middle of a monologue and there was no budging him until he clued into the nonplussed faces of the local forestry workers who were getting angrier by the minute.

It took the police a long time to arrive, having to physically remove all the debris on the road approaching the blockade, and by the time they arrived, they were in a foul mood. There were at least a dozen cruisers and police vans; the first cop to appear wielded a video camera and another officious cop pointing a finger at each demonstrator to be carried off. Blockaders were taught to resist using passive resistance only, going limp when officers carried them off. What pissed off the cops was the fact that they had to climb down into the log barricade to hoist out the blockaders, one-by-one, amidst a barrage of shouts to "save Temagami pine forests." Luckily, most granola-munchers were vegetarian, lightweight greeners, and were easy to extricate from the structure.

While I was taking photographs for the TWS along with the photographer and writer from the *Toronto Star*, we were given the finger by the official OPP officer in charge of pointing out those to be hauled back to the cruisers. We were escorted to a cruiser and shoved in the back seat. There we sat for the duration of the arrests, for more than three hours. Cops would stride by the window drinking cold pop while we were given no water and no breaks to take a piss. Bob Rae was also arrested, along with another fourteen blockaders, and finally driven to the town of Elk Lake to be "processed" and released. All those processed were warned not to participate in further actions or they would receive sterner punishment and an arrest citation.

As the days progressed, the arrests increased, and the level of blockade action deteriorated. Cops were getting smarter while blockaders, running out of ideas and ways to create disturbances and work slowdowns, were failing to make much of an impact on road progress. At first, blockaders were successful at locking onto machinery, the cops taking up to three days to figure out how to cut through kryptonite bike locks. Two or three activists would lock on while at least one other person would work as "assist" to the blockaders attached to machinery in case they needed food or water. Trouble is, the assist would normally carry the keys for the bike locks. It didn't take long for the cops to figure this out, make a quick arrest, confiscate the keys, and release the locked-on blockaders, who were subsequently arrested.

Then there was Paul. Paul was arrested at least three times and was the most creative when it came to causing problems for the cops. He carried in a bag of quick-set cement one morning and buried his bike lock in Portland, deep in an excavation in the middle of the road. Unfortunately, the cops were there long before the cement hardened and hauled him off for the last time.

Blockaders losing ground on the earthbound tactics began taking to the trees. But some blockaders were more interested in appearance in front of the media than worrying about tactical protocol; we lost our four-hundred-dollar tree-climbing spikes when a zealous activist donned a bright red jacket, walked into the action site thick with police, and was hauled off before he had the chance to strap them on and get up a pine tree. Marika did get up a large pine at the frontlines and stayed there for thirteen days, having to endure smoky fires and threats by loggers wielding chainsaws, not to mention living in isolation at the top of a seventy-five-foot tree in near-freezing weather.

Having set up the camp and provided canoes, tents, water purifiers, and other supplies, it was my job to either fly in or paddle in to periodically check the condition of the blockade base camp. Usually it was a mess, and water purifiers were haphazardly abandoned and half-buried in the beach sand, blockaders opting to dip their cups directly in the shallow bay water.[2] Someone had brought in a forty-five-gallon drum and propped it up on rocks so that it could be fired underneath and the drum used as a communal bathtub. It was popular, but nobody thought of changing the water;

---

2. Shallow beaches typically carry the highest threat from contracting parasites such as giardia, or "beaver fever"; after the camp dismantled, several blockaders did get sick from drinking bad water.

they would simply reheat the water that was in the drum and hop in with a friend. When I saw it, there was a thick layer of grey sludge on the surface.

Anarchy prevailed, at least for the duration of the blockade camp. Despite our best efforts to run a successful campaign, and to base operations out of a remote wilderness camp, there were no rules, no organizational infrastructure, and no plan at the front line. There were heroes, of course, and individuals who devoted their time, efforts, and passion to a worthy cause. But even anarchy needs a working paradigm to succeed ... and a leader.

The blockade is a facet of the evolution of the environmental movement, where best efforts are gauged and judged by the reaction of the people at large, which in turn is controlled entirely at the whim of the press. For the Temagami Wilderness Society, the blockade can neither be hypothesized as a success or a failure. It was costly, in terms of dollars, and to the personal lives of all those involved in such an undertaking. There were 344 arrests over the eighty-four days of the Red Squirrel Blockade; thirty of the protesters faced fines of up to five hundred dollars or twenty days in jail. In the bitter cold of November, when the bays and creeks were freezing over, the camp could no longer be run effectively or safely. The road construction progressed steadily and without conflict.

On November 11, the chief of the Teme-Augama Anishnabai, Gary Potts, flew in to the blockade camp, thanked the few souls remaining, and told them that their job was done. The TAA would take over and move the camp to the road at Sandy Inlet to the east where it could be maintained by motorboat until freeze-up. The government now had to deal with the Natives, on the road and in the courts.

In the late 1980s it was not difficult to recruit crusaders willing to devote time and effort to such causes, or to even participate in a wilderness-based blockade. The environment then was a big issue, worldwide, and the global movement spiked because of the loss of prime old-growth forests. The pervading mindset of the 90s, after everyone started feeling comfortable about global affairs, polarized a collective shift to lifestyle and job security. And even though the 2000s saw a marked increase in awareness to big issues, like global warming and the continued loss of life-sustaining forests, it would become almost impossible to stage a successful blockade today. Financially, legally, and psychologically the idea of a road blockade as a measure of defiance and a feature of environmental action would fail before it began. Industry and government control the media, and unless wilderness crusaders are being crushed by road-building bulldozers or logging skidders, the green action isn't sexy enough to gain the favour of the press.

When John and I got back to the base camp on Wakimika, there were still several blockaders sitting around the communal firepit. Somebody played a guitar; another sang to the chords — Dylan or Young, it was hard to tell what song they were trying to sing. A joint was being passed around. Some had fallen asleep by the fire, curled up on top of life jackets, spooning newfound partners. Sounds of lovemaking in the tents had long since diminished, exchanged for sleep noises, snoring, farting, coughing, and tent zippers unzipping by dull-headed greeners looking for a place to piss.

John flipped our canoe over and slid it into the calm water of the lake. We paddled the half kilometre to our campsite on the north point where we had pitched our tent away from the main camp. We were tired and had accomplished nothing save for a brisk walk along a new logging road.[3]

A loon called in a faraway bay.

---

3.   After the blockades in 1989, the Bear Island Band and their demands for a settlement in their land dispute became a hot topic and the Red Squirrel Road was deemed "too political" during court proceedings. The road was formally closed by gates which by no means kept out sportsmen on all-terrain-vehicles.

Ingrid Zschogner.

4

GEE HAW!

Have you broken trail on snowshoes? Mushed your huskies up the river, Dared the unknown, led the way, and clutched the prize?

— Robert Service, *Call of the Wild*

There were nine anxious huskies in the back of the Chevy Blazer; two or three were spilling out over the front seat, exploring the back of my neck with salivating jowls and probing noses.

"Geez John, where's your trailer … it reeks like a canine brothel in here!"

John curled his moustached lip into a wry grin and I knew what the answer was — the axle broke, the tongue snapped off again, or something. And here we were, driving along an ice road, three hundred feet above the bottom of Lake Temagami, arms busy restraining crazed animals and rubbing drool and steam off the windows, all while attempting (with modest desperation) to keep the eggs I had for breakfast in their appropriate place and not in my lap.

These were friendly dogs though, hardworking mutts who have an innate habit of pissing on each other (or down your boot when your back was turned); amiable travelling partners but disgustingly offensive to the olfactory mechanism. I supposed after a few days of communal living with these creatures in the wild, that I wouldn't smell much better.

I was anticipating a little man–dog bonding anyway; I knew the more I got to know these huskies the less faith I would have in my own race. People were complicated, narcissistic, and unfaithful. Dogs, on the other hand, live an unstructured life; all they have to do is sleep, eat, piss, crap, pull a man-sled on occasion, fight for canine posterity once in a while (the political pecking order was uncomplicated), and look cuddly for the tourists. Reincarnation as a dog isn't an entirely dreadful thought. Not a blue-collar working dog, mind you, but a pampered and groomed lap-mutt or porch dog. I've tasted dog food before — I could get used to it.

The musher, Pete Moss,[4] was an outdoor adventure entrepreneur; having been born in the North gave him a colloquial edge and he had the Northern diction down to a fine art. Not in a disparaging sense, he had that "mountain-man" aura that southern-bred and wannabe guides have to work hard to project. Clients loved him … and sometimes, when he could get away with it, he loved them back. He was married, sort of, when it was convenient. He had to be admired; after all, not everyone could do a handstand atop a racing dogsled.

Moss had been hired to run my winter dogsled program back in the early 90s. I didn't realize how much room forty dogs would take up, or the amount of poop they would manufacture, or the noise they could make. He had been running dogs commercially for four years and was good at it. He treated his dogs well (unlike some mushers) and he put his heart into it. It's all about tolerance, something Grey Owl knew something about: "Dogs are still beaten to death in their harness by their owners, and so-called sportsmen. Willing to take a chance which only animal will have to pay for …"

Me, well … I was a veteran of the dogsled misadventure. My bruises were still healing from the last outing, but at least I was learning how to stay on the sled, use the brake when I was supposed to, get off and push on the upslopes, and use my body weight to lean around obstacles on the narrow (and often harrowing) bush trail.

The dogs know when you screw up, too. Deviating one iota from what they know to be competent handling will cast half a dozen discordant,

---

4   Not his real name.

over-the-shoulder looks and "get your act together" barks. Personally, I just have trouble, mostly, with trying to remember their names. It's a good thing dogs don't really mind; out in the beyond they could very well hold a grudge if there was such a thing as dog protocol. I had Pete draw me a schematic layout of the team so I could attempt to memorize their names: Blaze — the lead dog — then Trapper, Duke, Cor, Badger, Czar, Monty, Clay, and Eli trailing behind.

My earlier introduction to dogsledding culminated in a kind of embarrassing and potentially pain-rendering mishap. I was the last of three sleds, packing out the gear from one of our bush camps. My load had become disarranged so I stopped my team to fix the problem. Now, dogs do not just stop on command; all they want to do is run, especially if they see the lead sled disappearing up ahead on the trail. That's where the snow brake comes in handy. It's a grappling hook-like claw that's fastened to the rear of the sled by a two-metre line; hoofed into the packed trail snow it's supposed to keep a jerking dog team securely anchored. In theory it works with perfection. In practical application there are a lot of variables: the strength and determination of the team; how well you kicked in the brake; consistency of snow pack, et al.

I could have snagged it to a sapling, but I didn't want to take the time. That was a mistake. I was standing there, trailside, getting rid of three cups of morning tea, when all of a sudden my brake released and off went my team to catch up with the others now far ahead. That should have been the end of it; an embarrassing hike out in the least, but it wasn't to happen. The liberated snow hook precariously attached itself to my boot lacing, flipping me unceremoniously onto my back (my nylon anorak acting as a super-slider).Ricocheting like a pinball from tree to tree, I was dragged by these hyperborean hounds down the worst trail this side of hell.

At the time I was more concerned about being found dead with my fly down, so after that corrective procedure, I concentrated on extricating myself from the snow hook before my leg was pulled out of its mooring — permanently. Luck comes in strange ways sometimes, and the sled jammed against a tree momentarily, giving me the opportunity to yank the hook off my boot before the dogs sped off again down the trail. I swear, if dogs could laugh, that's exactly what they were doing as they disappeared.

"O, what men dare do! What men may do! What men daily do, not knowing what they do!"

Shakespeare. He knows all about humility; like catching up to your runaway dogsled while everyone else looks on in amusement. Professional adeptness, I learned, is the ability to catch up to your dogs *before* anyone else sees you brushing the snow off your hindquarters. Now I understand why Pete always held lead-team position. If he fell off (which didn't happen often, or at all as far as I can remember) he would just command his dogs to stop. Our own teams obediently followed close behind Pete's, manoeuvring through forest, across frozen lakes, almost mindlessly. One of the most frightening experiences I had as heal-team was when I went through the ice with a full team. We luckily had enough momentum and strong dogs to pull us out of trouble.

Pete did all the shouting: "Gee" for pull right; "Haw" for pull left; "On-by" to keep a straight run through confusing intersections; a commanding "Heeyah!" or "Hip-hip!" to get rolling — and often *"you sonovabitch, asshole, motherfucking, stupid mutt,"* when one of the dogs chewed their way out of its leather harness.

Sometimes he would even get in a fight with one of his "rangier" dogs, or, to break up a fight, bite their nose or ear or other body part to smarten them up. Pete figured that his dogs would respect him more (in a totalitarian, Alpha-male, dog-regime way) if they looked at him as the "dominant" part of the pack. It seemed to work. Sometimes he would walk away from doing battle with blood on his face or hands, which totally freaked out the women clients (until social hour in the lodge at dusk when the primitive man became the focus of female attention). Nonetheless, if I were ever to get in another bar brawl, I'd like Pete to be there — even if it was just to watch him latch on to someone's nose with his teeth.

Of course, you have to wonder, as I did often, what would happen if I were alone, just me and the dogs and the lone trail, if perchance I were to fall off my sled. Would the huskies just keep traipsing off, setting their own course … forever? Or would they feel sorry for me ten kilometres later, maybe come back, pick me up, and laugh, as dogs do.

The ice road terminated just north of the village of Bear Island, treaty home of the Teme-Augama Anishnabai — and none too soon. The fresh air outside the vehicle was a much welcomed change. The dogs were restless to get going. It was snowing hard. Heavy stuff, the kind that blots out shorelines and obscures packed trails. We were heading in to my cabin, about forty-five kilometres to the northwest, and trying to locate a historic nastawgan (aboriginal) trail that was used to access the Lady Evelyn River up until the 1940s.

We had one sled and nine of Pete's best huskies. They would be pulling a week's worth of gear, Pete on the sled and me on skis riding behind. Each dog had to pull its own weight of thirty kilograms and a total of over a quarter-ton of men, equipment, sled, and dog food. Two weeks before, I had hauled in a load of food and supplies by snowshoe and cached it behind a cabin on Diamond Lake, at the halfway point. Not an easy task in and of itself. The trail in was anything but flat. After parking the Blazer, we set up the team as quickly as we could.

The dogs kept up a constant speed of seven kilometres per hour, sometimes losing the trail because of the snow buildup. Pete would occasionally halt the sled so that he could check a couple of the dogs' feet for embedded clumps of snow packed between the pads.

We passed familiar points Sealrock and Raccoon and crossed Devil Bay and Granny Bay, but stopped short at the narrows into Sharprock Inlet, where there was open water. This detour added at least an extra five kilometres to our journey north to the Red Squirrel Road, but the dogs had a better trail to run on.

The road was hilly, so Pete and I eased the load on the upgrades — Pete running alongside the sled and me skiing glide with a slack line. The downside was fast and furious and the sled sometimes buried itself in the deep snow off the side of the trail.

The going was tough on Diamond Lake; there was no trail and the snow was deep with sections of slush that bogged the team down considerably. Water eased up through the runner tracks. Once at the outpost cabin, we chained off the dogs. They looked as if they had just taken a walk around the block. Pete and I literally collapsed by the fireside, sipping on brandy and massaging aching leg muscles.

In the morning we trimmed the weight down because we didn't really know what conditions lay ahead. I left on skis ahead of Pete to break a trail up the lake through the deep snow because I knew the dogs would labour in the slush. Pete caught up a half-hour later and we had hot tea beside the Anishnabai rock paintings. I continued to break trail, but on snowshoes this time, making it easier for the dogs. We bushwhacked for at least a mile, coming upon unexpected pitch-offs and barriers that had to be circumvented; trees and deadfalls were cleared with an axe. It soon became apparent that this was not part of the original nastawgan route. It took us four hours to punch through to Willow Island Lake.

Pete's team, also pulling my pulk, stretched for sixty feet — it was a nightmare task trying to coerce a nine-dog team through a tangled forest full of snags, pitfalls, and steep rock outcrops. John had broken the handlebar off the sled, but kept going; I put my skis back on, but my feet were soaked by this time; we were both exhausted. The sun was near setting and we picked a spot on an east shore across from the old nastawgan route to make camp, just so we could enjoy the last few minutes of sunshine.

Pete tended the dogs while I pitched camp and cut firewood to last two good fires; we needed to dry out our clothing and boots before heading upcountry to the cabin at the falls. It was a clear, cold evening with good promise of fair weather for the hard work coming up. We would leave the dogs at the camp and break trail for five kilometres, then return to camp by late afternoon.

Breakfast consisted of fried bacon chunks, grease, oatmeal with maple syrup, and a lot of tea. With a day pack we struck off, expecting to reach the cabin without any problem. I broke trail with Pete following behind, cleaning the trail of snags. There was scant remaining sign of the old trail except for overgrown blazes; it looked as if fire and age had obliterated most of the trees that were marked, replacing it with thick undergrowth. We had to bridge several creeks with cut spruce — a time-consuming task that ate up most of the afternoon. After three kilometres we returned to camp. The slush on the ponds we crossed would freeze solid overnight and make a tight trail for the dogs.

The dogs were glad to see us, immediately howling to get fed. They eat first, with no mind to our own weariness or needs until they are looked after. Exhaustion sets in once you start to think about it. It was dark by the time we were set for the night. The two candles in the tent raised the ambient temperature to a comfort zone that broke the chill and the fatigue, but conversation thinned out quickly as we realized we were more tired than we were willing to admit to each other.

Snow. There was a gentle pattering on the tent fly as if mice were dancing on tiptoes and then sliding down the sides of the tent. We dressed in a hurry, John looking after the dogs while I cooked the last of the bacon over a fresh fire and warmed up milk for the oatmeal and dehydrated apples. The camp was left intact for the return trip, leaving behind the pulk and unnecessary gear. I had to walk the three kilometres we had broken the day before, as the trail was still too rough for the dogs to haul two passengers. It was snowing steadily but not heavy enough to obscure the view ahead. When we reached trail end, Pete chained off the dogs and we set off for the cabin on a new trail.

The snow was deeper here, powdery without much buoyancy; snowshoes sunk to the depths, getting tangled on underbrush and tree snags. The two kilometres quickly turned into three as we veered south to bypass a steep cliff dropping off to the Lady Evelyn, following a small creek bed draped in overhanging cedars that eventually brought us out to the canyon below Twin Sisters Falls. Slush oozed up through the snow on the river edge, making it all the worse for travel. There was open water at the base of the falls. Standing mesmerized at the river sculpture that rose up before us, the vault of sepia-toned ice encapsulating the falls stood like a great cathedral. The portage trail around was steep and icy, and there was no easy way up. Once at the top of the cliff, the trail levelled out all the way to the last stretch back to the river where we ran into bad ice along the shore. More bushwhacking.

With the cabin now in sight, strained leg muscles pumped the remainder of the adrenalin needed to make it up the last high ledge of rock to the cabin, above the next falls. Pete dumped his pack and headed back downriver along the now broken trail to tend to the feeding of the dogs while I fired up the cook stove and made dinner. Pete would have to walk the three kilometres back to where the dogs were chained and heat up enough water over a fire to mix with the dry dog food, then hike back to the cabin before dark.

It took a while for the log cabin to warm up. About four feet of snow had to be dug out even to get in the doorway, and once in, the temperature was colder inside than out. Before the air was in any way temperate, every frozen object had to thaw and heat up. I hung up our wet clothes to dry and propped my mukluks by the side of the wood stove.

"*You're in rough shape, shaganash,*" whispered a man's voice from the dark corner of the cabin. The oil lamp barely distinguished any features of the man save for the deeply retracted eyes and braided hair tied off with rawhide thongs. It was Owl.

"*Jeezus, Archie, why do you do that every time? Why don't you just knock on the door like normal people?*" I knew it was a stupid question and he wouldn't bother me with an answer.

"*You're out of shape, winded. I watched you both as you came up the river.*" Owl moved into the light and took a stool near the stove, holding his long-fingered hands over the stove to warm them up. "*And you let him break trail.*"

"*I've been sick,*" I said.

"*Yes, lovesick you are, like a fool. She left you, didn't she? What's her name?*" Archie asked.

"*I don't want to talk about it.*"

"*You let it break your will ... make you sick inside, weak. I know.*"

"*Of course you would know how I feel. Pony did the same thing to you at Temiscouata, and later at Ajawaan.*"

"*Yes, she did, but the time was coming, I knew in my soul. I couldn't hold on to the lie any longer and I didn't want her to be near me when it came down,*" murmured Owl.

"*Well, I'm not a charlatan like you, Archie — just a hopeless romantic.*"

"*See how far that got us, eh, shaganash,*" laughed Archie.

"*It would never have worked between us,*" I said. "*We weren't compatible — she was Capricorn and I'm a Libra.*"

"*I don't believe in that tripe,*" answered Archie, waving a hand to dismiss it.

"*What are you talking about, Owl? You're practically a mystic ... what about all the Indian stuff about the sun and the moon, totems and such?*"

"*That's different. Indians don't relate to the sun and moon phases in that stellar sense. You are what you are.*"

"*I don't agree. Look at Pony ... when was she born?*"

"*June 18, 1906.*"

"*Okay, that makes her a Gemini. When's your birthday, Owl?*"

"*September 18, 1888.*"

"*Shit ... Virgo. Archie, the only thing you had in common was the fact you were both born on the same day.*"

Archie looked up, puzzled.

"*You see, Archie,*" I said. "*Gertie's a masculine positive sign and you're a feminine negative sign — no match at all.*"

"*I don't follow,*" answered Archie, a little annoyed now, shifting uneasily on the stool. He lifted the lid on the wood stove and threw a piece of wood in.

"*See, she's just like the whiske-djak, the trickster, playing tricks, always moving. Pony was a jack-of-all-trades; she picked up things quickly, right, Archie?*"

Archie nodded his head.

"*Well, whiske-djak gets bored easily. Gertie wanted variety in her life, new experiences, new people. She didn't want to retire like you, Owl — not to mention the fact that you drank too much.*"

"*She wasn't very patient,*" Owl lamented.

"*Yeah, Archie, that's because you took too long. And you're an efficiency expert and that would drive anyone crazy.*"

"*I still don't believe you,*" said Owl.

"*Believe it, Archie. Why would she want to stick around and watch you write yourself to death. What was in it for her?*"

"*Well, it was her whole scheme with the beavers. If she didn't want to stay with me, at least the beavers should have been enough to keep her at Prince Albert.*"

"*Archie, the park and the media took over the beaver, and you were turning it into a sideshow. Pony was pushed aside, not by anything you did, it just happened.*"

"*So what's your excuse, shaganash?* Archie boomed. "*You're lady was twenty years your junior … nineteen, wasn't she?*

"*Same age as Pony was when you met her, and you were thirty-eight.*" I answered.

"*Archie, tell me, it was just lust with you, wasn't it, with Gertie? It wasn't for the intellectual conversation, right?*" I probed, knowing I would hit a sore spot. "*C'mon, truth, Archie, what more could it be? You were just a horny guy flaunting your charm when you met her at Wabikon Lodge.*"

"*It was different then,*" Archie answered.

"*What makes it different?*"

"*Honour, shaganash, honour — a thing of the past now, in your time. But I was an honourable man all the same,*" Archie said, squaring his shoulders and sitting up as if the extra height would give him some semblance of moral support.

"*Honour?*" I said. "*What, do you mean that you didn't sleep with her up Abitibi way, the winter she shacked up with you? Is that what you mean by honour, and who would believe it if you said no anyway, Owl?*" I questioned. I had been there, in that so-called "honourable" dilemma, paddling for months with my first wife before we were actually married; we were good friends, not lovers, but nobody would believe that we hadn't shared a bed.

"*It was like that, or nearly so, for a while anyway. We had to be careful, but, yes, she was a beautiful woman,*" bewailed Archie.

"*Sure, Archie, she was a beautiful young girl, and beautiful young girls have romantic notions that soon grow stale with age in a very short time; then they just want security, a house, and a low-maintenance husband. Men tend to be more romantic as they grow old. Archie, it was a flash in the pan relationship, just like mine. We should have known better. But again, lust or even the prospect of love with a much younger woman is like firing your gun off into the night sky and not knowing where the bullet will land.*"

"*Then why can't we forget them? Why do we do such harmful things to ourselves over the failed love of a woman? Look at yourself. Where are you in your life, shaganash?*"

"*I'm right where I want to be, Owl, here at my cabin, where I don't have to answer to anyone.*"

Owl stood up as if to leave, paused, and looked around the cabin.

"You know, I've been here before the cabin was built, and camped at these falls in '26 when I guided the lads at Camp Keewaydin. And I knew that Newcomb fellow and his partner Horr when I was at Bear Island in '08 when they paddled to James Bay and back in five weeks time. Everyone sure praised that man.... Strange way to end it, though — chopping up your wife with an axe and slitting your own throat. I was in Ajawaan at the time but it was big news in '34. I kept in touch with a couple of Temagami friends when I was out at Prince Albert. I sure missed the pine country here."

Archie's voice faded; the crunch of footsteps outside the cabin.

Pete had returned from feeding his dogs. When he had arrived at the place where we chained them up, the dogs were nowhere in sight. At first he thought the chains had broken and they had run off, but they had simply lain down and allowed the snow to blanket over them. Dinner had stewed in the oven and I fried up a bannock as a complement, all washed down with strong bush coffee, thick and bitter (somewhat like my ex-wife), Pete all the time talking about how his marriage wasn't working and me falling in to the same conversation with a particular zest, about women, and luck ... or bad luck, and how the next time around will be better, and why is it that women don't have any staying power, and it's really all about money, or lack of it which is mostly the case. And freedom; how good it feels to be on the trail, camped in a log cabin fifty miles from the nearest road. The evening was rife with philosophical banter and "what-if" repartee.

Leaving at dawn the next day, it didn't take us long to backtrack on the packed trail, harness the dogs, and reach our tent camp by mid-morning. The tent was dismantled, and we loaded up all the gear and struck off, this time in a new direction, south to a small procession of lakes that would take us more directly to Diamond Lake. The route we had taken in to get here was not practical, even though we had broken a trail already. It was too rough, still, and the new route looked promising.

It was a good decision. Two short but steep trails needed only a light packing and little brushing because of the big pines and sparse ground cover. Because the trees were enormous, they weren't subject to windfall or age, the nastawgan blazes were still visible, and the trail easy to follow.

The dogs were in good form after the day of rest, and pulled hard and strong, even with me short-roped behind Pete and the sled full of gear.

Instead of camping on Diamond Lake, we kept up the pace into the evening, turning west and south along an old forestry logging road where the trail would be packed and the dogs would have an easier time. There was no prospect of a moon to light the way, and we still had thirty kilometres to go over hilly terrain. But no moon is needed in the winter; there is always enough light to illuminate the path ahead as the snow seems to glow with a spectral radiance, and any deviation in the pitch of the trail is relayed by the movement of the dogs.

Up and down, up and down, for five hours, pushing and gliding over rise and fall, the dogs never faltering or slowing their pace unless the brake was set and tea was called for. Bodily functions were always done on the run, the doer nimbly hopping on three legs for a piss and a running squat for a dump. For me it was a quick side-step on the skis if I felt a fresh movement approaching.

Rest time: a quick fire is kindled by the side of the trail and the tea-pot hung over a prop-stick; dogs panting and smiling, sniffing and nipping at each other, a chorus of barks and howls, but always on the move, impatient to get going.

Sounds: the heave and mingling of dog breath and padded feet on hard snow, the smooth hiss of the nylon sled runners over the trail, and nothing else but the music of motion, stars aglitter, and the dark silhouette of trees against a darker sky. "Hiyah!" Pete would yell on the long uphills, running alongside the dogs, encouraging them to pull their best with the promise of double rations at the trail's end.

The lake appeared ahead as a white void with no discerning shadow or contrast or depth, a slight downslide at trail's end, and it would be smooth sailing all the way to Bear Island down the northwest arm. Lights appeared in the horizon. The dogs, sensing they were close to the end of a hard day, started to relax in their harnesses, and Pete would give a friendly command to keep going. And they did, of course, all the way to the Chevy Blazer, unrecognizable under a heavy fall of snow.

I was tired. And the paroxysm of lost love that hung like a night mist on my soul was lifted. That's what the trail does; it purges you of guilt or grief or longing and opens the door to fresh thoughts and aspirations. I thought of Grey Owl, made frail by war and worry, wearied by heavy toil for years on the trail, retired to Ajawaan and Beaver Lodge, only to live and love vicariously through his books and lectures.

The Blazer ploughed over the ice road through fresh snow; a husky lay his muzzle on my shoulder and sniffed my ear. It was Clay, the heal-dog, strong, friendly. He licked the side of my face as if to tell me everything was all right.

Grey Owl had a particular fondness for working dogs and a respect he often only showed to "men of the trail." Of the husky, he wrote, "Lean, rangy, slant-eyed and tough as whalebone, hitched in teams of four; over muskegs and across frozen lakes; tails up, tongues hanging, straining against the harness, bracing themselves at the curves, trailwise and always hungry, these faithful animals haul their loads all day for incredible distances."

5

EASY RIDER

The instinct of nearly all societies is to lock up anybody who is truly free. First, society begins by trying to beat you up. If this fails, they try to poison you. If this fails, too, they finish by loading honours on your head.

— Jean Cocteau (1889–1963)

The boat listed to the starboard side dramatically, enough for the vehicles chained to the deck to teeter on two wheels. Floating motionless for a few seconds, partially suspended, chains taut but looking conspicuously pathetic, the two trucks and four cars would thump back on the deck, time and time again, after each wave. It was unnerving. The motorcycles had long since fallen off their kickstands, stopped from skidding off the deck and into the ocean by a light chain. Icebergs would appear through the fog, ominously close, grey and menacing. Dave and I just looked at each other and said nothing.

A man stepped out of the hold, gripping the handrail as the boat swayed, and made his way toward us.

"Ya bys er from Untario, I see by yer plates." The man grinned. We nodded.

"Better watch yersefs on the Brador side, by the Jeezus."

"Why, what's up?" Dave and I answered, thinking this was some kind of joke building up. Newfoundlanders were proud of their ability to crank a chain, especially if it dangled from a mainlander.

But this was no joke.

"Don't get settin' yer eyes on any village girls, cuz the last bloke from Untario got hisef beat up real good." The man's expression changed to one of admonition. It was a known fact that the girls from northern Newfoundland and coastal Labrador tried earnestly to latch on to boys from out west. They would do anything to escape the old-world life.

"Nobody's ever brung sickles across the straight afore ... makes folk a might nervous, ya know." The man eyed the fallen bikes and shook his head and walked back toward the hold. He stopped and turned around.

"And where's ya gonna ride anyways... aint no roads, just caribou tracks up the coast."

Then the ocean got rough.

Next to canoeing, motorcycling was an easy second choice as an avenue of escape and a source of adventure for me. I was riding at age fourteen and had already been reprimanded by the constabulary for riding under-aged without a licence ... and without footwear ... and sometimes minus a helmet. Some of the things I would do on a bike defied any sensible notion. Later, as riding mates perished in rear-enders, or got T-boned by drunk drivers (most just lost a leg at the knee), or pasted themselves against a rock cut when they couldn't make the curve at 120 miles per hour, I had smartened up enough to realize my own limitations.

Dave was a biking friend who worked for Pegasus Helicopters. We would often ride together on weekends, up to Quebec or the Southern Townships, or through rural Ontario. We biked up to Mont Tremblant and snuck our motorcycles through the gates of the Formula One race-track just before a race. The track was famous for its tight, banked corners, and Dave had this obsession about riding his cycle around the course. So we did it ... with course patrol car in hot pursuit.

Dave rode a 750cc Honda 4-stroke, while I straddled a 750cc Kawasaki 2-stroke, or blue-fog machine — a fast, light bike that needed a faring mounted on the front frame to keep it from doing wheelstands off the mark. Not your environmentally sensible choice of wheels, but when you're twenty-one, the road or trail was paramount and the environmental movement wasn't a conscious thought in anyone's minds, except for a handful of west-coast hippies. And we biked at a time when biking wasn't exactly socially accepted — at least on the roads — and we had a time of it with the jaundiced attitude many drivers had of bikers.

Dave and I weren't your typical chain-wielding, Harley-driving, Hell's Angels bad boys ... just two independent souls looking for an occasional escape. And we certainly found adventure one summer in 1974 when we decided to bike to the east coast and across to Newfoundland and Labrador.

So, with camping gear and a modicum of clothes strapped to the passenger seats of our motorcycles, we left for Montreal from my chicken shack residence north of Toronto in the late afternoon. Just outside of the city we chanced upon a carload of girls sitting off to the shoulder of the road, waving their arms for us to stop. They were on their way to their parents' cottage in Vermont, about a two-hour drive south of Montreal. Their muffler was dragging on the ground and it took about fifteen minutes to fix with a strand of wire I kept in one of the faring pockets.

That act of chivalry bought Dave and me a couple of free nights at their cottage. But sitting on the dock in the sun, even bikini-clad girls soon lost their charm, and we struck off, heading east through the backcountry of New Hampshire and Maine, sleeping off-road in woodlots wherever we could punch our bikes far enough off the main highway. We hit heavy rain in New Brunswick and spent much of our time under the cover of overpass bridges, soaked and tired, aspiring to catch the Newfoundland-bound ferry out of Cape Breton by evening. With only minutes to spare, we arrived in time to board, and quickly made our way to the topside lounge for drinks.

While Dave played the one-armed bandits (and subsequently won enough change to pay for his trip), I staggered to the lowest floor in the boat and splayed out on a couch in the steward's ward, my stomach doing cartwheels from the slow surge and swell of the ocean. *Christ, sea-sick ... that's crazy ... I spend half the year in a boat, bobbing up and down in lake waves and crazy rapids.* The beer and pizza sloshed around in my stomach in sync with the ocean. I had passed up a canoe trip for this adventure and I was beginning to think that this motorcycle trip was a bad idea.

Archie was sitting at the bar drinking Johnnie Walker Red.

"*What are you doing here?*" I queried suspiciously. My stomach had settled somewhat and I ordered a ginger ale. I didn't drink much at all until this trip, and the alcohol had made me stupid and sensitive to the ship's movement.

"*What, do you think all I do is paddle around, write speeches, save beavers?*"

Archie had that gleam in his eye, the look just before he does a jig, or one of his contrived war-dances, or plays the piano. *Oh no, he's going to make a scene,* I thought.

Instead, he spun around in his seat and looked out the window at the moonlit ocean.

"*I like the ocean, shaganash; and in those last years, I spent more time crossing the Atlantic in steamers going back and forth from England than I did in a canoe. That's the sad part. But I like the ocean because it's a different kind of wilderness; there's none of man's atrocities visible to the eye here.*"

"*Oh, yeah … you should see the amount of garbage they throw overboard into your wilderness, including the toilet waste,*" I added. Archie just shrugged.

"*I could get used to cycling,*" Archie said smugly.

"*I thought I left you behind.*"

"*Why should I let you have all the fun? Anyway, you seem to need a good poke every once in a while.*" Archie beamed.

"*How kola, shaganash … and good luck.*" Owl slipped away, holding on to his glass of Johnny Walker, trying desperately not to spill his drink as he step-danced down the hall and out of sight. He'd show up at the craziest times, unannounced and usually unwelcome. So, Grey Owl, I read your book *Pilgrims of the Wild* last year when I wintered on Diamond Lake. I didn't care for it as much; it was a bit sappy and not at all like your first book, *Men of the Last Frontier.* That had real character — it wasn't a love story like *Pilgrims.* Women and booze were newly acquired interests, neither of which I knew much about nor could handle with much prudence.

Upon reaching Porte-aux-Basques in the early morning, a typical Atlantic fog had enveloped the landscape, obscuring everything except the larger road signs. Here the east coast winds were known to blow railcars off the tracks; but it wasn't windy at all and we laboured to keep the bikes centred on the road. I was hallucinating, which happens on a bike quickly if you don't have full visibility and you're over-tired. We pulled off at a sign advertising a mountain lodge and followed the rough blacktop for several kilometres until we came to a tidy little mountain inn. We signed in, took a motel room, and slept for the rest of the day.

Bang, bang, bang on the door.

Now what? It was now evening, but still light enough to see that our bikes were safe in the parking lot. At the motel door stood a small assembly of folks. One was holding a large tray of food and another pushed two paperback books at me. As soon as I opened the door they stepped into the room, sitting on the edge of the bed, the chairs, and the dressers, making themselves comfortable. Dave and I just rubbed our eyes trying to make sense of it.

"We seen yer bike plates were from Untario ... just thought we'd welcum ya to the rock and all," a big man said. "And ta show ya that we make fun of us folk here, we brought ya some good reading hare."

I looked at the books; volumes one and two entitled *Book of Newfie Jokes*. The food was exquisite — homemade breads, fresh salmon steaks, and a couple bottles of Newfie Blue Star beer. We chatted for a while and exchanged salutations, but not before one of the older gentlemen suggested we drop in to meet his daughter who happened to be our age and quite handsome. We thanked them for their generosity and watched them pull out of the parking lot and disappear into the fog.

It was here then that we learned of the peerless character of the island's people. We sat in the lodge bar at our own table, some distance from the crowd that had now collected. It was customary in Ontario to create and guard your own space when you sat at a bar; small clusters of drinking folk segregating themselves from others, for the most part not socializing except by circumstance. Dave and I were almost physically carried across the pub floor and perched in the centre of the gathered throng and set up tidily as the focal point of conversation.

"No one drinks alone here, by," someone said. And that was it. Conversation was thick, mostly about who had the fastest snowmobile that could outrun the local game warden.

"The last one got tossed in the river wrapped in a salmon net ... nearly died he did." That was Carl; he built remote cabins along the upper river for a few bucks and sold them to American fishermen for $5,000. Thing is — he didn't own the land, but everyone knew he was doing it, and they all drank a round in his favour for putting one over on the Yanks.

We worked our way up the west coast the next day. The north highway was not paved, as we soon found out, and we laboured over rough cobble underlay that was being dumped for the new road surface. It was tedious work, crawling along loose rock, beating off hordes of blackflies that descended as soon as we stopped for road graders.

When we finally hit hard-pan gravel, we let it out past Cow Head and the Arches, stopping only briefly, camping on the beach under a swath of tuckamore and listening to the waves rolling in off the ocean. We were to catch the ferry at St. Barbe which would take us across the Strait of Belle Isle to Blanc Sablon and Labrador. The tide was in, so the ferry deck was sitting almost three metres above the docks. There were two narrow plankways set on the dock used as a ramp to get vehicles to the deck of the boat. Vehicles already on the boat had left a slick of greasy mud on the ramp boards so there was no room for mistake. There was a space of about six feet between the boat and the dock, and the surface of the water was covered with Portuguese man-of-war jellyfish.

Dave went first, taking a good run at it, and made it up safely. I didn't know if I could make it up with my bike and I hesitated too long. *Hesitation kills...* was a slogan on a bumper sticker I had seen in New Hampshire. I had a racing bike, not a low-geared touring cycle; any deviation off the vertical would throw the balance off because of the weight of the packs on the back. I had one shot at it.

The back tire started spinning just as I neared the top of the ramp and I could feel my balance being compromised. The front tire slipped over the edge of the ramp and locked on the deck, but the back tire only spun. I was in a real fix. Three beefy dock hands stood on the deck with their arms folded, enjoying the entertainment, not moving.

"Grab the fucking bike!" I screamed and the dock hands finally scrambled and grabbed on to the front forks of the bike, hauling me the rest of the way up the ramp.

The locals were not friendly here, like in the south. I could tell they felt uneasy about us bringing motorcycles to the port, and then getting on the boat to go across the strait. They probably wondered why anyone would want to go unless they worked there; few tourists ever came up the long coast road. The boat pulled out of the harbour once the vehicles were loaded and chained down. *Chained down?* The captain told us they had lost trucks overboard, on occasion, even after being chained down. We thought he was joking.

Everyone stood at the rails: garbage was tossed overboard; pop cans, chip bags, dirty diapers, you name it, it all went into the ocean. Ten minutes later, once we broke the port bay and entered one of the roughest straits in the world, only Dave and I were left on deck. Icebergs on both sides of the boat; the swells were big enough, now we had to dodge icebergs, as well? We made it to the hold and sat on a bench with the rest of the folk. Nobody looked at us or said a word. The boat zigzagged crossing the strait in order to avoid colliding with the ice.

When we reached Blanc Sablon we couldn't see a thing because of the fog. Lourdes-du-Blanc Sablon was a grouping of three tiny fishing villages at the cusp of Quebec and Labrador with an overall population of just over a thousand people. The nearest village to the west was Côte-Nord-du-Golfe-du-Saint-Laurent, and to the east, up the coast of Labrador, was L'Anse-au-Clair. People were dependent on the lobster and salmon fishing, and canning puffin and harp seal meat. Tourism didn't happen until twenty years later when the fisheries went for crap.

Hotel Blanc Sablon wouldn't give us a room. They said they were full and to go away; we knew that the hotel was empty of patrons. The proprietor at the variety store — a transplanted Islander who spoke English — suggested we leave our bikes in his back shed, otherwise they'd get smashed or stolen. I parked the bikes while Dave made arrangements for us to bunk in with two of his Pegasus Helicopters buddies who flew the chopper for the hospital. We had intended to camp somewhere along the coast, but the fog and rain dampened any thoughts of sleeping out on the barren heath.

First thing Dave's work chums did was to warn us to stay low. We could join them in the bar that night but had to sit with them and talk only to the imported nurses; in no way were we to make eye contact with any of the local Sablon girls. The last Ontarian to visit the village was almost killed for attempting to dance with a Sablonite female. No arrests were made.

It was a run-down pub stuck on the end of the Hotel Sablon. The wooden floorboards creaked and groaned underfoot and the walls were plastered with aging photographs of fishing boats and hunting excursions. Tables and chairs were cheap auditorium-style motif and the lighting was purposely subdued. It looked as if some of the men had been there for some time. *Don't make eye contact.* We sat with the Pegasus pilots and a couple of the nurses. A brand new juke-box lit up at the far end, playing Herman's Hermits, and several young women assaulted the dance floor with a variety of step-dances. Some of them cast eyes our way.

"They just got hydro power here last year," one of the Pegasus fellows whispered. I didn't know if he was serious or joking.

"They loaded the juke with Stones and Zeppelin but only do the traditional dances."

Young local boys sat grimfaced at the tables, sleeves rolled up, showing off flexed biceps, rarely looking at the girls on the dance floor; they were more interested in watching us. There had been an exodus of girls from the village, usually latching on to visiting salesmen heading back to the island or farther east. Ontario was their prime choice of destination, so the local chums were doubly cautious of our intentions. Word had gotten around quickly that two Ontarians on motorcycles had arrived on the boat earlier that day.

We survived the pub night, letting the Alpha village males rule the roost, then managed to ride our bikes up the coast as far as the glorified reindeer track would allow, into Labrador, just to say we had been there. After three days we felt we were living on borrowed time, made a hasty retreat back across the strait, and headed south. Torrential rain forced us to take a room in a run-down motel at Cow's Head. No heat and no hot water. We shoved our wet clothes between the mattress and box spring of the beds, hoping it might help to dry them out.

A van from Ontario pulled in and took a room beside us: five girls and one haggard male driver piled out. He told us he had picked the girls up in St. Anthony and they wanted a ride back to Ontario. It turned out none of the girls had any money and he was scared shitless his wife would find out, so he pleaded with us to take at least two girls with us. We declined the offer and left the man in his misery.

Gros Morne had not yet risen to high acclaim as a hallmark destination for tourists, mainly because of the unpaved north road. Only about ten kilometres had been paved, some distance up the arm, a test strip of asphalt where punks would come from miles around just to squeal their tires and drag race with their friends. The rains had cleared off and we managed to slow our pace enough to hike a newly stationed but only partially constructed boardwalk into Western Brook Pond. The Long Range Mountains stood up in the distance — one of the few places in the world you can see the uplifted Earth's mantle. It was not yet a National Park or UNESCO World Heritage Site, but Newfoundlanders appreciated the importance of the tablelands as a tourist draw. The landscape was pure Arctic tundra with no trees; the iron-rich, brown rock was peridotite, which lacked the nutrients needed to spawn even the most tenacious mountain life forms. It was also a toxic landscape, as the rocks contained huge concentrations of heavy metals.

Crossing at Woody Point on Bonne Bay Fjord, we stayed at the village of Bonne Bay for a couple of days and hiked the tablelands. Bonne Bay was a successful marine depot with a population of more than seven thousand. The fjord was stunning, with wooded coves and sand beaches, backed by the uplifted tableland panorama. There were no hiking trails built yet, anywhere, except for the short section of unfinished boardwalk back at Western Brook Pond. The barren landscape was easy to traverse except through sections of broken rock and scree on the steeper slopes, but the summits were relatively level. It felt good to work the legs after days of riding. It wasn't like canoeing, where you tax every muscle in your body, paddling and portaging and doing camp chores every day.

The adventure continued: rounding the island to St. John's; the ferry across to Cape Breton; the two girls in Cheticamp who had hitchhiked across Canada from Calgary, and who survived by stealing groceries and bumming rooms in exchange for carnal services; the seedy hostels we stayed in — brothels for the weary, unattached, impoverished self-seeker; near collisions with drunk drivers and jaywalking moose; pretty island girls who promised to write.

Home. Home? I didn't have a home in the real sense. Except for my bike, my tent, my canoe, and an illegal cabin up north; home was either the road or the trail. Freedom.

I took the train up to Temagami and paddled in to one of my favourite lakes. Blueberry season had come and gone but there were still saskatoons if you looked hard enough — a sweet and sour addition to a bannock fried over the coals. Newfoundland faded into the cerebral library.

My independence was self-determined by keeping to a rigid, inflexible tenet that prescribed freedom as a personal mantra. Archie Grey Owl was partly to blame. It was always about "the trail," and the ability to disconnect yourself from the things that are destroying mankind by destroying Nature. Grey Owl was obsessed with freedom; freedom from the responsibility of love and obligation as a husband and father; freedom from the pressures instituted by society — fear of conforming to some kind of mainstream dogma. This was a creed I had adopted and consolidated every time I stepped into the canoe, searching for lost rivers, or straddled my motorcycle and headed for the backcountry.

Archie, you had it easier than me; Canada was still in the making and men of your brand still found a niche. For me, born out of my time, it is too late to survive a dream that's only partly real, and to me alone. I am happy only on the trail. And the trail then, as Grey Owl would elaborate, "is not merely a connecting link between widely distant points, it becomes an idea, a symbol of self-sacrifice and deathless determination, an ideal to be lived up to, a creed from which none may falter. It obsesses a man to the utmost fibre of his being, the impelling force that drives him on to unrecorded feats …"

6

SPORE

Well, we had our first argument, you and me, and I suppose we both learned something.

— Grey Owl

There are those people in our lives who have helped define our character in some significant way. Be they good experiences or bad, they have perhaps added a bit of colour to the monochromatic path we sometimes follow. Friendships bonded in youth can be ephemeral relationships and, as it seems, old friends fall back into your life often when you slip into middle age. Nostalgia becomes a part of your psyche. It's a comfort thing, like a security blanket; but all you want to do is convince yourself that past deeds and camaraderie had a purpose in the bigger picture.

Grey Owl knew well how the toil of the trail can bond men together: there is something indefatigable about that kinship borne of hard work shared as equals; and like men standing in the trenches, bayonet's fixed and ready to fight or die, life on the trail with its vagaries and risks also cast men as brothers.

Spore and I went to high school together. His actual name was Soren, a new kid from Denmark, and we hung out. His father was a professor of chemistry at the University of Toronto; so, coming from a purely analytical patriarchal family, Soren, too, had scientific leanings. That set us apart, philosophically, so we shared outdoor adventures together as friends; canoe trips and winter treks happened often, sometimes extending into month-long sojourns. Deep, emotional conversation seldom happened. To Soren there was no God, and birds sang because their gonads were swollen and they were in pain. I was the romantic. Birds sang because they were in love, or some such thing. Soren was in need of a nickname that befitted his compulsion to explore the complexities of the natural world in finite terms, so the word spore came to be his handle.

At twenty-one we wintered in the bush together, up in the wilds of Temagami, and this was after spending months on canoe trips in Algonquin Park since leaving high school. Spore went on to university to major in ornithology; I pursued an art career. In the following years I saw Spore on few occasions, usually during one of his study projects to which I would offer my assistance. These projects always turned out to be life-threatening experiences, or, in the least, an adventure of gargantuan proportions.

CAMP 86

In order to earn his degree, Spore had chosen to do his thesis on the life and plight of the boreal owl of northern Ontario. But, like any of our adventures, this one had its resident difficulties. Although relatively common, the boreal owl is the least observed by birdwatchers in North America; the reasons for this include its size, ability to blend with the natural environment, its soft, unassuming call, and its location in unpopulated areas. So, with these traits in mind, Spore had made his choice based on the element of isolation and adventure ... not to mention the challenges involved.

Spore first located a couple of owls while on a winter camping trek on the myriad logging roads south of Highway 11, near the town of Opisatika in northern Ontario. He had befriended the boss of a logging camp and was invited to stay in the half-empty bunkhouse. Enticed by the cheap home-cooked (and substantial) meals in the cookhouse, Spore took up the offer gladly and made Camp 86 the base camp for his studies.

I visited him briefly during the spring of 1974, driving up on my motorcycle but staying only long enough to scope out his project, camp out, and help run some transect lines through the bush. What I remember well were the blackflies. I was used to camping and had had to deal with blackflies in the past, but the intensity and persistence of boreal bugs was enervating. Spore's dedication and passion to his thesis overrode the debilitating effects of the biting insects.

But what stood out on that visit, and haunts me to this day, is of the beautiful girl standing out by the edge of the long gravel road on the way in to Camp 86. I was compelled to stop for no other reasons than curiosity and the fact that she looked distressed and so out of place; I wasn't in the habit of stopping to flirt with girls, but our eyes had met as I passed her on my motorcycle, long enough to induce the need to find out more about her. I turned around and stopped. She had been crying. Her house stood just off the back road in various stages of decomposition and neglect. She was in her late teens and still dressed in what looked like hand-me-downs; but her eyes had this hollow, dejected, and penetrating look, beautiful but sad, longing and scared. She said she lived with her father, who worked in the bush. Beside the house were relic trucks, a backhoe, and a skidder, all rusted and decommissioned. I didn't ask where her mother was. She asked where I was going and I told her, and she smiled weakly when I mentioned that I was helping a friend catch a boreal owl. I don't remember her name but she asked me to look for her on my way out.

Three days later, when I stopped on my way out, the house was empty and she was gone. There was a deeper story here, somewhere, that was not unfamiliar to the plight of northern youth trapped in a nowhere life. Who did I think I was — her knight in shining armour, about to whisk her away from an obviously banal existence?

Later, in November, Spore called and asked for my help to catch a boreal owl. I was more than willing to help. The canoeing season was over and this would be the last adventure of the year. We arrived at Camp 86 on a Friday, when most sawyers and crewmen had gone home for the weekend or were in Kapuskasing spending their paycheques on women, booze, and gambling. Adam, the camp caretaker, and Bob, the cook, were still there and again welcomed the both of us to stay in the bunkhouse.

Camp 86 was one of dozens of bush camps owned and operated by Spruce Falls Pulp and Power Company out of Kapuskasing — the corporate big brother and biggest employer for the community. There was always a negative side to one-industry towns, a side not commonly shared within the community, but in this case the daily business of cutting down Ontario's boreal forests had far-reaching consequences. Spruce Falls Company had two major clients — Kimberly-Clark and the *New York Times*, both mega-consumers of Canadian pulp and paper. The surrounding boreal forests provided a ready source of wood fibre, just so Americans could blow their collective noses, wipe their arses, and read their daily papers. The forests being eliminated for these functions comprised the largest visible clear-cut from space telephotography — the devastation of the rainforests of Brazil paled in comparison. Black Spuce — the prime species being cut — grew to a diameter of no more than the thickness of your arm and were more than two hundred years old. The immensity of these forest cuts was never more apparent than during my second visit to Camp 86.

Initially, the camp was situated in the midst of lush spruce forest for miles around; but in the span of only a few months, the camp stood as a lone monument in a vast landscape of stumps and slash. Spore wondered about his previous studies, when there was nothing but thousands of square miles of deep boreal forest and he had success in taping the calls of the owl. Now there was nothing left but a few token stands, like small islands on a huge lake.

But in 1974 there was virtually no environmental movement; Greenpeace had just been formed and was making some headway on the west coast, but the plight of Ontario boreal forests would not become an issue for another three decades. Neither Spore nor I really acknowledged the ramifications of such intense forestry from a larger perspective, except that it might have an effect on his studies of the boreal owl at Camp 86. I was more inclined to object than Spore, having recently gotten involved in Temagami issues focusing on saving Maple Mountain from development, but I said nothing.

The camp staff had always been accommodating. During my first visit to the camp, operations were in full bloom and the dining room full of famished loggers. And in a logging camp dining room you are required to follow a certain eating protocol. Heaping plates of food were set on the long tables and it was a race to consume as much and as fast as you could within a few minutes. If you didn't keep up, you either did without, or the cookie would scoop up your plates for the wash before you were finished. The dining room was clear of men who had eaten the feature meal, downed pots of black, boiled coffee and homemade pies while I was still politely halfway through the first course, cookie standing over me with his burly arms crossed and face scrunched into a grimace of impatience.

During the work week, after sharpening their saws and tending to their field kits, the men generally went to bed early. Alcohol was not allowed in the camp, and for good reason. Sawyering is one of the most dangerous occupations known. And these men were professionals; what they did on the weekends was another thing, but during the work week, they were focused on the job ahead.

Spore certainly was a curiosity in the camp and most loggers respected what he was doing but were sceptical about the existence of a "boreal" owl. Most had had some experience with owls, mostly larger owls like the great grey, horned, and even snowy owl; but the boreal owl was a mystery to them, almost as much as the man who wanted to catch one.

One night the loggers were caught in a great show of past deeds and miscalculations while on the job. Safety was often compromised by taking chances, being in a hurry, or taking the chain-break off their saws. Spore had witnessed a contest as to who had the biggest chainsaw scar. Pants were dropped and shirts yanked up to expose the ragged, ripped flesh scarred by steel teeth, some old wounds extending the full breadth of chests or from ankle to kneecap. There was no accomplishment of bravery here, like war-wounds, or fighting bulls, or even a bar fight after sticking up for your girlfriend … just a show of self-effacement and mild guilt for not paying attention to the job.

The men were mostly of French Canadian extract, along with some Poles and a couple of Japanese sawyers who could no longer find work topping trees in British Columbia so they had moved east to Ontario where there was always work available.

Spore was surprised to see the extent to which they had cut around the camp, but it didn't deter him from going ahead in his attempt to catch a boreal owl. To catch one we first had to locate it, which in itself proved to be interesting. Spore had contrived a bownet trap that looked very much like a lawn chair hinged together with a large coil spring, like a mousetrap, only much bigger. Netting is attached to the U-shaped frame while the trigger is attached to a live mouse which is covered in dry leaves to attract the owl by making rustling noises. The owl hears the rustling, descends on its prey, and sets off the trap. Bingo — one caught boreal owl.

I had no idea how this was going to play out. We drove some distance away from the camp in order to find a stand of spruce, parked on the side of the road, and got out into a crisp, moonless November night. Luckily it hadn't snowed enough to accumulate on the ground, but the temperature was nearing the freezing mark. Spore started pulling some rather bulky equipment out of the trunk of the car.

"Here, put this on," Spore commanded, handing me what looked like a backpack reel-to-reel tape player. It was heavier than it looked. He strapped on a receiver of some kind with a very long telescoping antenna, then attached a hand-held sound parabola — the kind used by Dan Gibson to record loon calls. The two of us looked as if we'd just landed from another planet. A truck went by and nearly drove off the road when they saw us. Spore played the recording of a boreal owl he had taped earlier that year — a soft, staccato call, rising in procession from low to high *too too too toos*, almost resembling the sound of a nighthawk descending. After four attempts at different locations we finally had a response. We stood motionless on the road, the tape continuing to play the sound of a boreal owl while the real owl answered with a piercing *skeew* call from nearby. In the next instant there was a wash of cold air on the back of my neck and a thud on the back of the recorder. The owl had landed on my shoulder, but only for a second, and then flown off. We set up the trap nearby, but had no luck catching the owl, and after two more site locations we decided to pack it in. We raided the camp kitchen before sleeping, each downing half a pie and a handful of fresh-baked cookies.

The next morning we were treated to a five-course camp breakfast, and exchanged philosophies with Adam and Bob, who continued to think we were both a bit crazy. We assured them that this was the night we would bring back an owl.

And we did just that. Having just set up the trap, we were barely back on the road when we heard it go off. Spore ran in with his flashlight while I grabbed the cage out of the car. The owl was tiny, flapping its wings excitedly as we looked on in disbelief; it was still clutching the very dead laboratory mouse. In the cage it had settled down, and by the time we returned to Camp 86 it was so quiet we thought it might be dead. Adam and Bob were still up and they were as excited as us to finally set eyes on a boreal owl.

We left for Toronto the next morning and I sat for nine hours with a beautiful little owl on my lap on the ride back. Now that the adventure part was over and I had time to think about what I had just done (not accomplished by any means) I had misgivings concerning the welfare of this wild creature we had just stolen from its home. Oddly enough, Spore and I were both enthralled and mesmerized by owls: he with the *Aegolius funereus* — that tiny, robin-sized nocturnal hunter, and I with the *wa-sha-quon-asin* variety Indian wannabe. While Spore captured his prize in the name of science and the glory of being the first to find a boreal owl nesting site, I was trying to emulate the other Owl's lifestyle of adventure and solitude.

"You helped steal o-koo-hoo from his home," a voice chimed behind me. It was Archie, as usual, showing up every time I felt guilty about doing something.

"I was helping a friend ... so what?" I tried to be stoic.

"They'll put the owl in toilet paper rolls and wind tunnels and stick bands and receivers on its legs," Archie said.

"When did you become such an expert?" I retorted weakly. I actually silently agreed with him.

"Anyway," I continued. *"You took beavers from their homes and put them on display ... what's the difference?"*

"It wasn't for science. It was for their own good. Beavers were almost extinct if you remember," Archie said. He was right.

"Also, my shaganash friend, why didn't you speak out for the forest that's being cut down?" Archie was on a roll. *"And your friend is an authority on habitat destruction but he remains silent."* I hated it when he was right.

Now I really felt guilty, helping steal an owl for science, and staying at a logging camp where the boreal forest was being clearcut and wouldn't grow back for two hundred years.

Nineteen seventy-four was the year I started drinking.

EATING LOON

Pukaskwa National Park had just been inaugurated into the Canada Parks system and encompassed a good portion of the northeast coast of Lake Superior, from Marathon south to the east sweep toward Michipicoten. Spore had landed a one-year contract to carry out an avifauna study for the Feds and was stationed on a quiet, secluded part of the coast in Oiseau Bay. Once again he had asked me to come out and visit for a few days and I took him up on his invitation. Two years had passed since the owl escapade and Spore was now cohabitating with Margaret, a fellow ornithologist.

Spore picked me up in his boat in the coastal village of Marathon. The town was abuzz now with activity related to the new park and the commercial fishing season, while prospectors hit the local pubs and tourists milled about aimlessly. The bay was calm but Spore had warned me that there were huge swells on the open water and the ride would be rough. That was an understatement. The boat was small and Spore handled the motor from the back, taking each wave at full throttle, crashing down over the crest and into the trough and up and over again and again. This went on for almost two hours until we reached Oiseau Bay.

Lake Superior is one of the more dangerous bodies of water in the western hemisphere. The water is always cold, winds can lash up waves that rival any ocean tempest, and miles of sheer rock shoreline make it impossible to land a canoe or boat. It's also steeped in Anishnabai myth and legend. I truly thought I was going to die out on the lake that day, and when we landed, Spore told me then that just the week before he had capsized his boat and barely made it to shore, having to spend a cold night on the coast until he was rescued the next day. Having my ass pulverized on the hard wooden seat and not being able to walk for two days was a welcomed price to pay; at least I was still alive.

Spore and I not only didn't share particular philosophies about Nature and life in general, but we had disparately different ways of applying the skills of survival, from the art of building a shelter, to what we ate and how prepared we were. There was also the matter of respecting the elements, which seemed to be lacking in his tenets of good woodsmanship, although he did excel at not killing himself. Spore often threw caution to the wind — like the boat ride — and applied the "band-aid" approach to fixing things that went wrong. I had already learned that this philosophy doesn't work well over time because you can only tempt fate for so long before you get caught. I had screwed up myself and had enough life-threatening experiences already to know that circumspection and, in the least, a modicum of caution, is good practice. The boat ride terrified me because I wasn't in control of the situation, and said nothing because I wanted to trust that my friend knew what he was doing. It was like getting in a car with a text-messaging drunk driver and pulling out onto the Don Valley Parkway at rush hour.

Once my sea legs had repaired themselves, we went exploring the coast, but I had refused to go anywhere again unless it was calm. The adventure unfolded. We tracked down woodland caribou on the islands just off the coast; we surmised about the purpose of the "pukaskwa pits" — circular hollows bolstered with rocks — and walked miles of coastline. Canada Parks had just initiated the construction of the coastal hiking trail and it wasn't going so well, according to Spore. Most workers never showed up for work, or were so drunk they couldn't perform. There was a support barge following the crew along the coast; *sweet job*, I had thought at the time and contemplated signing up for work on the trails.

I didn't expect Spore and Margaret to have to feed me, although they offered, and I well remember what his diet consisted of on past trips. In high school we were always amazed at what he had brought for lunch; chocolate bar sandwiches or raw fish, when other kids were eating peanut butter and jelly sandwiches on Wonder Bread. And then there was the road-kill stage when anything recently hit on the highway was taken home and cooked up. On a month-long canoe trip we did when we were sixteen, we had run out of food; Spore had brought along a package of Gaines-burgers dog food (even though we had no dog with us) which he quickly consumed, saying that it was good and cheap enough to live on during our next trip — a trip I declined to go on.

Spore had called me up just before my visit and said that he was worried about the fish he had caught and eaten raw. The trout were easy to snag with a pole and wire hoop just by walking alongside any creek flowing into Lake Superior. Spore was used to dissecting animal and bird feces, including his own, and he soon noticed a multitude of tapeworm eggs in his stool. He worried about this for some time until he had himself checked out at a clinic. The clinic discovered that the eggs were actually undigested sesame seeds which he was using regularly in his baked bread.

Armed and forewarned about his eating habits, I had supplied most of my own victuals and hid them in my tent. But we did eat fresh pickerel, supplied almost daily by a commercial fisherman who had a habit of mooring his boat offshore and sleeping on the beach. He would scoop out a depression in the sand, line it with plastic sheathing, and cocoon himself out in the open, rain or shine, and sleep until dawn. A generous man, he would often gift Spore and Margaret with fresh-caught pickerel. Being a devout mainlander of English stock, I had refused to eat the fish raw, and so it was cooked, much to the chagrin of my Danish, seafaring friend.

The fisherman came in one day and, as usual, dropped by to chat. This time he had something different in his gift bag — a loon. It had been caught almost two hundred feet down in one of his nets. He thought Spore would want it as a specimen to study. He took it gladly ... except his intent was not to study it, but to eat it for dinner. To his credit, Spore wasted nothing, finding a use for things other people would cast away.

A dead loon really has little value for anything other than perhaps mounting in a museum or its waterproof skin used for a pair of moccasins — or, apparently, a meal for a crazed Dane with no food aversions. Any diving bird or duck was shunned by hunters and taken only in desperate measures. Fish ducks, like mergansers, taste like fish (apparently) and so would loon — you would think. Having no recipe for loon, even in the famous *Northern Cookbook*, we decided to first boil it (after plucking it, of course).

This proved to be a mistake — boiling it inside the small shack. The smell was nauseating. No one could enter the shack without holding something over their nose. After about an hour we guessed that the meat was cooked and sampled a piece. It was true; there was one recipe for cooking loon that I had forgotten about. To properly cook a loon, you first throw a rock in the pot with the loon, and when you can stick a fork in the rock, you throw away the loon and eat the rock. The meat was unpalatable. Not wanting to waste the bird, it was decided that we would cut the meat up in pieces and curry it into a stew.

I love curried dishes; it is one of those recondite tastes that stand alone. Add loon meat to this ambrosia and you have something resembling swamp, dead fish, and wolf musk. Even the look of it was disgusting, taking on a hue somewhere between bile and vomit, with the texture of rubber. Spore ate most of it, attesting that it "wasn't so bad," but complaining of a stomach ailment later that evening. Margaret and I tasted only enough to commit to memory one of the most unpleasant tastes imaginable. I can now admit to having eaten loon — a magical, prehistoric bird that should have received a decent burial.

MOPERT

Canada Parks constructed an interior base in Pukaskwa National Park. It consisted of a small, pre-fabricated ranger's cabin and an air-dropped A-frame research hut. Spore and Margaret had moved into the hut to carry on their avifauna study in the interior of the park. I had promised to ski in to visit them while they were there, but I had left it too late in the season; March had come in nasty, and by the time my new wife and I arrived in White River (branded the coldest place in Canada ... no wonder the town wasn't growing) it was pouring rain.

The only way to access the interior was by way of a rough logging trail that ran from the Anishnabai village of Mopert, thirty kilometres north of White River. If we were lucky, snowmobilers would have packed a decent trail and the going would be relatively easy. Staying the night in White River to wait out the rain and talking to the locals didn't convince me that this would be an easy trip.

"You're going to Mopert?" the old guy said. "You're crazy ... they hate white folk there. They get fired up and shoot their rifles into the provincial park across the river every once in a while. And last fall they tore apart some boxcars parked on the rail line, just for firewood."

It rained through the night.

By the time we drove to Mopert the rain had turned to drizzle and then light snow. Just outside the village we had stopped and jump-started a truck for some band men who thanked us profusely and gave us an address where we could park the car during our trek in. They also offered us a dog team to pull our gear the fifty kilometres in to where Spore was camped in the park. We declined the offer of the dogs, but did find the house and left the car and keys with the owner. I could only hope that my car would be there and in one piece when we returned a couple of weeks later.

All of our gear was in two backpacks and strapped to a toboggan. We were taking in quite a lot of extra food and two bottles of wine for our stay-over, as well as snowshoes and skis. It was a heavy load and the conditions were not favourable, the wet snow sticking to everything in clumps and the toboggan having to be de-iced every few hundred metres. Not having packed a tent, we needed to get to a trapper's cabin about fifteen kilometres in, marked on a crude map Spore had mailed me.

That wasn't going to happen. We had only made about five kilometres before realizing there was only an hour left of good light to make camp. By sheer luck I found a partially collapsed log cabin a short distance off the road. It was no bigger than a double shitter outhouse but the roof was sound and there was an old stove that could be fired up with a little jury-rigging of the stovepipe. We cleaned out enough debris to set up a makeshift bed, and set the door back into place using the back of an axe as a hammer to bang in the loose nails on the hinges. The stove wasn't at all safe but it was serviceable, and served us well to dry out our wet clothes. We let it go out before falling asleep.

The snow had crusted up during the cold of the night. Things were tightening up; whatever was wet was now freezing, and the woods were full of sound. I was in a half-sleep when I heard them. And there was more than one. There was a great long wail that curled the hair on my neck as I sat up to listen. My first thought was to wonder if they could get inside, or even wanted to.

Wolves. And there was much movement around the tiny cabin, as I could hear them sniffing at the toboggan, pawing at it, and talking amongst themselves in low growls. Then they all pitched in, howling in their own primitive voice that carried across the small lake and into the dead forest beyond; a sound that is felt deep in the soul and not heard by ear alone. It went on for some time, and to sleep after this was futile. Another fire was lit in the stove while we brought the toboggan and the rest of our gear inside, sorted it out, and decided to take with us only the basic necessities in two packs, along with our snowshoes, and ski the rest of the forty-five kilometres into the park.

It had warmed up again, enough to start drizzling and turn the track into watery ice. It was tough-going, hard on the legs, but we pushed it as far as we could before the storm hit. *A thunderstorm in March!* It was too early to camp but we made it to the trapper's cabin just in time as the skies let loose a volley of hail and rain. The cabin was in poor shape; the bit of firewood left inside was wet from a leak in the roof above it, the smell was horrific, and it seemed colder inside than out in the rain. We both started to get a chill, but there was little dry wood anywhere. I loaded up the stove and poured some naphtha on it to get it to ignite quicker, scrambled to find my matches — taking far too long while the gas built up in the stove. When the match was dropped in there was a small explosion that shook the cabin and almost blew my head off, the initial blast singing my eyebrows and knocking me backward onto the cot. That was a stupid thing for me to do, and I had watched other slack-minded campers pull the same stunt at campgrounds to get their fires lit, with almost catastrophic results.

At least the fire was going, and we slowly dried out, sipping at the one bottle of wine we chose to bring, not waiting to share it with our friends. This trip was not panning out the way we thought it would, once again demonstrating the vagaries of late winter weather. With a warm cabin, a bottle of wine, a warm bed (pushed between the leaks in the roof), and the sound of thunder outside, we at least mellowed in the face of adversity, laughed at our circumstance, and knew that tomorrow would be different.

The temperature dropped to well below freezing overnight, and a skiff of snow covered the icy track. Perfect conditions for the thirty or so kilometres still to go, and we reached Spore's and Margaret's A-frame in the late afternoon, tired but elated. Upon arrival we downed several mugs of hot tea and fresh-baked scones. It was obvious that

Margaret had had an effect on Spore's recalcitrant habits; the A-frame was immaculate and well organized and there was even a spice shelf — and no dog food!

My wife and I slept in the vacant Parks cabin as there was no room in the tiny A-frame for four people. We stayed a week, exploring by day and night, enjoying the interior winter landscape of the new park, places few people will ever see, following lynx tracks by moonlight, standing at the precipice of a frozen waterfall, and enjoying the warm camaraderie of friends at the edge of the world.

We had the option of skiing out when the weather was co-operative, and managed to reach our cabin cache easily on the second day's travel back out, the only event being a near collision with three moose that had decided to bed down in the middle of the day at the bottom of a steep hill on the trail. With the ease of travel by ski, rather than by snowshoe, I had wondered if Archie had ever travelled this way. He seemed to be a man who would resist something new; impassive to change, driven by habit.

"Shaganash, don't you know anything?" Archie reprimanded.

"What do you mean?" I asked.

"Well, in my days up in Abitibi country or Bisco, we didn't have the good fortune to travel over well-packed snow-machine trails. We had to break our own trails by snowshoe … even for the dog teams." Archie was on a run.

"Yeah, I see your point. They say a snow-machine trail is equal to forty people on snowshoes," I replied. *"But skis are much faster,"* I told Archie, without being very convincing.

"Skis won't work in deep snow or thick bush, shaganash. I'll keep my snowshoes, thank you very much."

Archie was finished ... always the last word.

When we reached Mopert it was late afternoon. Our car was intact and recently washed of road salt and mud. Native faces peered out the window at us; young children, curious, imploring, smiling. We explored the car and our packs for gifts, and presented what we found to the family in exchange for having looked after our car. *"Migwetch,"* they said shyly; and we thanked them in return.

Friends come and go; some we stay in touch with over the years, others are cast off like unused clutter and forgotten. Spore and I bonded in high school, and started off on the same trail doing outrageous things together. We evolved and became less tolerant of our differences even though we pursued interests that embraced the natural world. But the natural world has scientific, social, cultural, philosophical, and emotional attributes, and the way people embrace the wilderness are as varied as the landscapes. I have more respect for this Danish comrade today because he stood true to his ideals, and we both softened at the edges of our respective ideologies, becoming more liberal in our expectations and judgments. He is currently a professor in the biology department at Acadia University in Nova Scotia, where he teaches ecology and conservation biology.

When Archie Belaney became Grey Owl, he removed himself to that sacred kinship of friends, the "Rivermen" as he so eloquently depicts in *Tales of an Empty Cabin.* Jimmy Espagnol, Zepherin, Mathewson, Billy Mitchell, all became characters in the lines of a book, lost in the trenches of Owl's own personal war — men who wouldn't quite understand the reasoning behind Archie's new persona. It was a great and terrible sacrifice Belaney made to sustain the deception and the cause, and no doubt a great source of pent-up anger and despondency. Coupled with Anahareo's departure, the loss of his friends, too, was cause for Owl's despair and heavy drinking. He couldn't replace the rivermen in Prince Albert; the park employees being pampered and preened by steady salaries and easy work were not of the same ilk as the men of the trail.

In *Tales of an Empty Cabin*, "Rivermen," Grey Owl writes, "All honour to you, old friend. Very well I knew you, better than perhaps you ever thought. And in the old days, whether we met over a glass of the best, or maybe to discuss some small point of personal conduct concerning which we could not, for the moment, see eye to eye, there was a mutual respect, and an ungrudging appreciation of the other man's qualities. And besides, it was all in the Game — the good old, sporting Game that is now so nearly played."

7

007 GREY OWL —
THE MOVIE

I thought Attenborough had fallen off his rocker.
— Pierce Brosnan, on first reading the script

If ever there were a story that would make a good movie, it's the story of Grey Owl. He was not only Canada's first noted conservationist when he fought to save the beaver from over-trapping in the 1930s, but he was also an enormous celebrity. His magazine articles and four books about the Canadian wilderness and his "beaver people" developed a huge international following. Dressed as an Indian, in fringed buckskins and moccasins, and with his hair in long braids, the Englishman gave lectures to packed halls on both sides of the Atlantic. In 1937, he even gave a command performance for the Royal Family.

When I severed the *extensor digiti minimi* — the main tendon that controls the movement of the index finger — it didn't bleed much. The visiting surgeon at the rural ER didn't really know what to do to fix it. The tendon recoiled like an elastic band, so I was told to pull one end out while the doc sewed it to the other end. It was a messy, painful job, but at least I was reconnected and could once again work my finger.

"How did you manage to slice your finger?" asked the surgeon.

"Throwing knives — practising for the new movie about Grey Owl," I told him, somewhat ashamed of the mishap.

"Who's Grey Owl?" the surgeon queried. I couldn't believe he didn't know who the Canadian icon was; but the surgeon, after all, was from Vancouver, on the other side of the Rockies, far removed from Grey Owl's stomping grounds.

I first heard that Hollywood was planning to make a film about Grey Owl early in 1998 from Dave Gorenson, the founder and executive director of the Rivers and Lakes Foundation of Canada. He called me up because for three decades I'd been a guide, park ranger, and outfitter in Temagami — Grey Owl Country — and I'd also worked as a wilderness consultant on several documentaries.

"Who's playing the part of Grey Owl?" I asked, biting my lip and picturing a buckskin-clad Mr. Bean waving a rubber tomahawk.

"Pierce Brosnan got the part."

Silence.

I felt nauseous. Remington Steele, James Bond *for Christ's sake*, playing the part of the man who inspired me to live a life in the canoe. This could not be. I imagined Grey Owl in a tuxedo, portaging a canoe or confronting an enemy trapper while flashing a Walther PPK pistol in his face.

"Grey Owl, how do you like your beaver?"

"Shaven — not furred."

No, no, no, *NO!* And it wasn't just the Grey Owl thing; there had been too many nauseating films produced about the Canadian wilds where prefabricated canoe paddlers couldn't paddle if their life depended on it.

I sent my portfolio to the producers and explained why they needed a wilderness guide from northern Ontario to teach Brosnan the Ojibwa or guide-stroke — the method of paddling Grey Owl learned from Michael "Big Feather" Mathias in Temagami. I could show him how to throw knives and tomahawks. I could even show him how to piss out of a canoe without ending up like Tom Thomson.

Several days went by. Then Jake Eberts, the film's executive producer, and the producer of such blockbusters as *A River Runs Through It*, *Dances with Wolves*, and *Black Robe* gave me a call.

"Pierce wants to talk with you," he said, "tonight. He'll call you."

Now what do I do? I didn't think it would actually get this far. I grew strangely nervous, as if I were waiting for a call from Grey Owl himself. But when the phone rang, the voice sounded, well, like James Bond. Brosnan called me "mate" with his slight Irish accent and poked fun at my suggestion that he "learn how to piss" out of a canoe (which he agreed to do). He wanted me as his personal trainer.

Grey Owl probably would have liked the idea of a Hollywood movie made about him; ego aside, it would be a sure way to spread the word about conservation. As a convincing actor himself, he knew as well as anyone that to get such a serious message across, you have to entertain people. Still, I'm sure he would have been as fanatical as I was to get the story more or less accurate. Jake Eberts, the producer, told me that the forty-five-million-dollar movie would be Pierce Brosnan's first chance "to really act." And it soon became apparent that Brosnan cherished this role as an opportunity to convince movie-goers that he could portray more than just a mock hero. He wanted to personify the "real" nature of the Grey Owl character, and I had something he needed — a Temagami fix, not just the skills, but a spiritual sense of the place that moulded the man. Eberts had told me that Brosnan keeps his trainers close during a shoot, for security, and that he always wanted to look good. He took his movie parts seriously.

But he didn't need me right away. He was shooting the movie's winter scenes in March and he'd already learned how to snowshoe while in Alaska with environmentalist Paul Watson — mutual friend and co-founder of Greenpeace. It was February, and I was booked to work with Brosnan in April. In the meantime, Eberts had mailed me a copy of the script to critique.

Sir Richard Attenborough had already brought the lives of Mahatma Gandhi, C.S. Lewis, Steven Biko, and Charlie Chaplin to the big screen. The story of Grey Owl had always intrigued Attenborough, and this would be his pet project. When the script arrived and I had flipped through the 117 pages, I had serious reservations about the validity of the film. William Nicholson was one of Attenborough's choice script writers. Having produced winning movie lines for *Shadowlands*, starring Anthony Hopkins, and later *Elizabeth* and *Gladiator*, he had now fashioned a story around the life of Grey Owl.

The opening scene had Grey Owl vaulting his canoe over a twenty-foot waterfall, coming out unscathed in front of the camera.

What the hell is this? I thought. It got worse. Black bears roam the forest in mid-winter, trappers harvest raccoons ... *has Attenborough lost it?*

"I like it." Archie's voice behind me.

"How can you like it?" I queried, almost angrily.

"People might think I would actually do something like that," Owl remarked.

"It's a cheap stunt, a Hollywood trick to sell tickets," I shot back.

"So, you're going to scuttle this then, tell Attenborough what you think?" Archie retorted, scowling and serious.

"It's not always about you, Belaney. I'm thinking of the general Canadian canoe culture. This movie makes a mockery of two Canadian icons — you and the canoe. Don't you see that?"

But he was gone again, as usual, showing up unexpectedly and leaving as if riding a breeze, tiptoeing stealthily through the shadows of my life as if still-hunting moose.

It was a whitewash. There were no shades of "grey" in Grey Owl at all. Nicholson had taken a potentially effervescent story and turned it into a pasty movie devoid of contemporary pith. There was no dark side, no drinking to excess or womanizing or bigamy or the abandonment of his children — just a pastel portrait of a romantic, untroubled, middle-aged, relatively normal soul. With Brosnan as key player, it's just James Bond in buckskins and braids.

I met Kirk Wipper at the airport in Toronto in February. Kirk was a mentor, in his late seventies, and a Canadian icon himself as the founder of the Canadian Canoe Museum. Eberts and Attenborough had invited us both to Montreal to meet and discuss the script. Wipper and I compared notes and noticed we had circled the same gaffes in the script. We agreed to speak our minds during the meeting with Attenborough.

The temporary home of Ajawaan Productions Incorporated was in an old warehouse on the south side of Montreal, a bit seedy but otherwise functional as a production office. Photographs and sketches of location sites, props, costumes, and scenes covered the walls. More props, architectural models, and binders packed with archival data were lying on tables. Kirk and I sat down with the production crew and waited for the director, Sir Richard Attenborough. My hand was still bandaged from the knife-throwing accident at home, practising for my stint with Brosnan in April. I told everyone that it was a "carpentry" accident.

Attenborough — an elfish, bearded seventy-five-year-old — was easily recognizable from his role in *Jurassic Park* as the man who built the dinosaur theme park. He's not intimidating, I thought, as he took a seat opposite me. And when he asked me for my impressions of the script, I didn't hesitate.

"The first scene is too Hollywood."

Around the boardroom table, the production crew took in a deep breath and waited for Attenborough's response. Suddenly, I couldn't believe what had come out of my mouth. But Attenborough just smiled sweetly and said, "Oh, we can't have that at all."

I thought he was going to start dishing out ice cream to everyone.

Then co-producer Diana Hawkins — who had introduced the movie idea to Attenborough a decade before — jumped in.

"This isn't a documentary, Mr. Wilson," she said, raising an authoritative brow my way. "It happens to be a Hollywood love story."

I could understand that, but I couldn't see the need to resort to cheap sensationalism, and I told them so. No self-respecting paddler would purposely push their fragile cedar-canvas canoe over a twenty-foot waterfall. Attenborough understood the value of authenticity and said that he would "fix it" — whatever that meant. I gifted him with a quartz stone taken from an Ojibwa tooling site in Temagami, and gave a talk and slide show about Temagami that he watched wide-eyed and glowing. He told me that he had listened to such a story about northern Ontario when he was eleven, and had attended one of Grey Owl's lectures in London in the mid 1930s.

"Are you ready to meet Brosnan?" Attenborough asked. I told him that once my hand had healed I would fly to Malibu to teach him his skills for the spring shoot.

Within two weeks there was a revised script. The opening scene now read:

1. EXT. FOREST AND RIVER, NORTHERN CANADA, LATE SUMMER — DAY

The mighty Northland: a vista of forested hills stretching away to the far-off mountain ranges, broken by the glittering shards of a thousand lost lakes. No roads or buildings, no signs of man. Only the eternal wilderness beneath the towering northern sky.

2. EXT. RIVER, LATE SUMMER — DAY

In the centre of the scene, a broad river runs TOWARDS CAMERA, and from some near but unseen source comes a deep and ceaseless roaring sound.

OPENING TITLES RUN

One moving point in the wide vista draws the eye: a MAN IN A CANOE, gliding down the river towards us. Too far off to make out any details, except that he handles his canoe well, with swift and economical movements.

Slowly, the SHOT DEVELOPS to reveal that the river along which he travels falls ahead of him down a long run of white water rapids: the source of the roaring sound. The river that seemed so tranquil is here transformed into a racing cauldron, in which through boiling foam we catch glimpses of rock formations twenty foot and more.

The CAMERA COMPLETES ITS MOVE, settling close to the surface of the lower river, beyond the rapids, where once again the water runs in a smooth and level stream.

The man in the canoe, high above but still IN FRAME, paddles himself almost to the edge of the rapids, and there skilfully holds his canoe in place, turning this way and that, while he inspects the dangers ahead. He and his craft look so small against the broad rapids it seems inconceivable that he will choose to follow the falling water.

But suddenly he gives a cry, twists his paddle in the water, aims his canoe directly at the lip of the fall, and with two powerful thrusts, drives himself down into the foam.

Now he has completely disappeared. From time to time a momentary flurry seems to mark his descent, but whether it's the smashed fragments of his canoe, or some broken branch being swept downstream, it's impossible to tell.

The TITLES RUN ON without a sight of the man and his tiny craft. How long does it take to run these rapids? Surely he must be hurled out by now, dead or alive?

But nothing emerges except the ceaseless tumbling torrent, which crashes into the lower river, and boils and swirls, and is carried away, calmed once more, past our point of view.

3. EXT. RIVER, LATE SUMMER — DAY

Suddenly, shockingly close, the CANOE BURSTS UP out of the water before us: with a yell of triumph, he comes hurtling AT THE CAMERA, paddle flying, powering himself to safety.

As he reaches the calm water he raises both arms and gives a call of pure delight, and we see him clearly for the first time: a lean man with a striking weathered face, long dark hair tied back in braids, worn buckskins drenched by the rapids.

ARCHIE GREY OWL, Indian guide and woodsman.

Eyes bright with excitement, breathing hard, he settles back down into his canoe and streaks OUT OF FRAME.

OPENING TITLES END

April: Fortunately, I had little problem passing a ski-bag full of paddles, throwing knives, and tomahawks through customs. Once the jet touched down in Los Angeles, a limo whisked me away to the Malibu Beach Inn. When I got there, dressed in non-formal, semi-guide duds, the desk clerk gave me the look of disdain. After I told him who I was he immediately changed his demeanour:

"Oh, Mr. Wilson, you have big friends here in Malibu" (meaning Brosnan, of course).

When I got to my room there was a chilled bottle of chardonnay and a hand-scripted note from Brosnan on a table beside the fireplace. I cracked the wine, poured a glass, walked out on the patio, and looked out over the Pacific Ocean.

This one's for you, Archie.

I met with Brosnan the following morning. He was dressed in faded blue jeans and a T-shirt, and was already wearing long braids *à la* Grey Owl, sewn in by a professional hairstylist from New York. His handshake could crush walnuts. He looked different without makeup — plain, ordinary, more like me. I felt more comfortable knowing he wasn't dressed in a tuxedo.

Brosnan's hillside estate had suffered irreparable damage from recent mudslides, so he and his girlfriend, Keely Shaye Smith, were temporarily renting Ted Danson's seaside condo (previously owned by Keith Moon of The Who), for a paltry sum of ten thousand dollars a month. Steve McQueen's old house sat vacant next door.

We sat in a sunroom overlooking the ocean and drank coffee. Brosnan apologized for Danson's "grotesque" furniture. He asked if I thought he was supercilious, pompous in my estimation. (Traces of insecurity?) I told him that I didn't know him that well except for his recent movies, and that my mother worshipped him as Remington Steele. We talked about the film, about Grey Owl's lifestyle, and mused about what he must have been like.

"I think Grey Owl was a man with an extremely complex nature — a tortured man, alone with his thoughts," Brosnan said.

(Archie rolled his eyes. He was sitting close by on the living room sofa.)

"This role is truer to Pierce Brosnan than anything I've ever done before." He told me that, like Belaney, he had been estranged from his parents as a child and was later shunted from one relative to another.

He asked me about Bear Island and the Teme-Augama Anishnabai.

"Things have changed," I said. "Temagami is being developed and I don't think Grey Owl would be too pleased."

"Maybe this movie will help," Brosnan said. "We need to save these wild places for our children." There was no pretence when he said it — just warmth, an honest, easy smile, and maybe a little sadness in his eyes. Back home I had been embroiled in the ongoing Temagami clear-cut logging issue and I imagined Brosnan to be the champion to support the fight. I was wrong. And his answer to my request would eventually put Brosnan and I at odds with each other and lead to my name being removed from the credit roll as his trainer.

Later that morning, Michael Grey Eyes, the renowned Canadian Cree dancer, showed up at the house. Since he was working in L.A., he had agreed to teach Brosnan some basic First Nations dance moves for a couple of scenes. We pushed back the couches and chairs in the sunken living room (Archie helped), and Grey Eyes loaded the CD player with a recording of war songs. It was the strangest scene; the three of us (as well as Archie who was enjoying this immensely) sweating profusely, shirtless, whooping and strutting like warriors, circling the living room, parading to the beat of the drums and a crescendo of chants.

After Grey Eyes left, Brosnan and I headed inland in one of two BMWs (courtesy of the manufacturer) he had in his possession. He lamented the fact that the Bond movies had been sponsored by BMW and he really would have preferred the classic Aston Martin coupe used by Connery, his 007 predecessor. We drove past his hillside mansion where the front slope had collapsed, exposing the foundation of the swimming pool. I told him there was nothing he could do to remedy the problem; anyone who had built on an unstable slope would be living in fear of a landslide every time it rained. Mudslides and wildfires were to plague the Malibu hills for years.

Malibu Lake was actually a flooded reservoir. Aside from the ocean, it was the only water body for miles in which to put a canoe in. A local outfitter had deposited a canoe at a cottage owned by a friend of Pierce's; the outfitter had already taken Brosnan out on the water for some basic skills. After letting him paddle a few strokes, I urged him to forget what he had learned. He was absolutely terrible, and the wind blew the canoe all over the lake. I sat up front, as ballast, facing Brosnan as he took the solo position.

"Pry off the gunwales," I told him. The canoe suddenly came under control and surged forward.

"Now dip the opposite shoulder and put your back into it. No! Don't look at your paddle — look straight ahead, beyond — use the thousand-mile stare."

I have to admit, 007 was a quick learner, and eager to be good at paddling a canoe. I enjoyed barking commands at him, and he listened. After the paddling lesson, I taught him "the walk" — to place one foot in front of the other like a fox, not splayed out like a white man. Throwing a canoe over his shoulder hurt his back, so we nixed the lesson and, yes, the pissing out of the canoe trick was also put on hold. We headed back to Malibu, picked up some sushi, and celebrated Pierce's newfound skills with champagne and a bevy of close friends.

There were no ugly people in Malibu. The wind had cut the next day's lessons short, so we stopped off and picked up cigars (not Cubans) and hung out. Women would wave Pierce down at the street corners and he'd always *coo coo* in his suave Bond demeanour. We drove through the hills, cigar smoke swirling out the sunroof, chatting about the Grey Owl movie. We ended up on the coast, at a memorial he had built for his former wife, Cassandra Harris, who had died of ovarian cancer in 1991. She was the mother of his three oldest children: Charlotte, a twenty-seven-year-old about to make Brosnan a grandfather at forty-six; Christopher, a twenty-six-year-old who once pounded out a pestering reporter while Brosnan looked on approvingly; and fifteen-year-old Sean. To honour his wife of seventeen years, Brosnan built a whale observation lookout on the beach and donated it to the people of Malibu. Brosnan stared out at the ocean, smoked his cigar, and reflected on his life. Although the death of his wife had hit him hard, he was now optimistic about the changes in his life. Winning the role of Grey Owl promised a new direction for his career.

"Life is good," he said.

We returned to his condo, and while Smith breastfed their son, eighteen-month-old Dylan Thomas, on the beach, I taught Brosnan how to throw knives. Tossing blades at a wooden support pillar holding up the house next door went well until the neighbour came out wondering who or what was attacking his house.

"They're not darts, Pierce, these are knives. Throw them like knives." I instructed with little success. He would have been more comfortable with an Uzi machine pistol in his grip.

Bron Roylance was Brosnan's personal makeup man. He was always with Brosnan, and I could tell they were good friends. Pierce kept him close at hand, whether he was on set for a movie shoot or not. The two of them were working on a remake of the movie *The Thomas Crown Affair*, to be produced by Brosnan; Roylance and Pierce were going over a list of potential leading ladies to star with him in the flick.

"Julia Roberts … no, she doesn't like me. How about …" Brosnan was verbalizing his list to everyone in the room, looking for feedback. A courier came to the door with a package, and Brosnan opened it enthusiastically. It was a gift box of cigars from his friend Burt Reynolds, with Burt's own brand name on them. Pierce gave me a couple to take home.

"Rene Russo … yes, she's the one … I'll give her a call." Brosnan was a workaholic; it was obvious he rarely took time out from the movie business. His wife took me aside and we chatted about how Pierce really needed to get away and would I consider taking him up to my cabin in Temagami. "Anytime," I said, thinking that if I could get Brosnan up to Temagami as a campaigner, the media ricochet effect would be terrific.

Hanging out with Pierce, smoking expensive Dominican cigars, cruising around in his BMW through the hills of Malibu, and occasionally talking about the film exemplified a lifestyle far removed from what I (or Archie) was comfortable with.

"I want you with me on the film shoot," Pierce had explicitly told me.

"Don't worry about Lenny — I'll deal with him," Pierce had promised.

Lenny Young was an aspiring, young assistant director to Attenborough; irritating and demanding, he had agreed to pay me a thousand dollars a day to teach Brosnan, but Malibu was to be the extent of the contract. I told Pierce that we needed to work on his canoeing skills some more if he wanted to look the part, and he agreed to have me at each of the shoots to take place in Quebec, much to the chagrin of Young.

The producers of the movie had considered Temagami as a location, but needing an active steam train and accommodation for the large crew, they opted to shoot at a number of places in Quebec instead. The political scene in Temagami was too hot, anyway, and the Quebec government was willing to cut the producers some slack as far as tax concessions, and to allow them to develop an elaborate site shoot in Mastigouche Park, northeast of Montreal.

At the end of April, I headed to the Marriott Hotel in downtown Montreal to meet up with Brosnan. After dinner the Brosnan entourage headed to a popular jazz club.

"It's not my kind of jazz," Brosnan admitted, and the band picked up on his disapproval. Pierce was smug and distant, as if he didn't want to be there at all and was just killing time. There were no paparazzi in Montreal, no fanfare for actors; Montrealers were used to Hollywood film crews and actors plaguing city streets and tying up traffic. Brosnan seemed to thrive on publicity, and the lack of media hype put him in a foul mood.

For the next three days, Brosnan and I met each morning at the grounds of Sir John Abbott College, on the shore of the St. Lawrence River, to work on canoe skills. When students, mostly teenage girls, recognized 007, he obliged their requests for autographs. He always had time for small talk. The girls giggled and asked if the long braids were really his own hair.

"Of course they're mine," he'd say. "Here, have a tug." In fact, the braids were woven into his hair and waxed in place over a period of time, a project that cost several thousand dollars, with a lifespan of about three months — just enough time to finish the movie.

Archie Grey Owl had spent hours working on his appearance: to look convincingly like an aboriginal, Owl would spend hours sitting in his canoe, letting the sun bake his face and the back of his hands brown like the Anishnabai, or rubbing a dye into his skin made from the pulp tannin of the inner skin of poplar bark, or pushing his nose down with a spoon, giving it the downward hook visage. Brosnan was starting to believe in the part.

By this point Pierce was comfortable in the canoe and a powerful paddler. We moved from Montreal to a lakefront house he'd rented in St-Gabriel, a small village located just south of the Réserve faunique Mastigouche, one of the chief shooting locations. When I arrived in the park there were over 150 people milling about the scene; a number of them were busy rolling brown paint up the trunks of flame-blackened pines after a carelessly tossed cigarette burned down the prefab cabin. The cabin had been an expensive prop with a removable roof and walls so cameras could zoom in on the love-struck Archie and his nineteen-year-old flame, Anahareo. The role of Owl's love interest co-star was played by twenty-one-year-old Annie Galipeau from Maniwaki, Quebec. Her mother was an Algonquin and her father Métis. One of five girls tested for the part, Brosnan had told me that Galipeau was chosen because "she was the best kisser."

Brosnan worked from five in the morning until eight at night. I would have short periods with him in which to work with him on his canoeing skills. He had the J-stroke down to an art, but he was stiff and awkward on the turns. He was also paranoid about falling into the cold water. After work we'd hang out at the cottage, spend the evenings throwing knives or tomahawks, or sit by a campfire by the lake's edge. I remember playing guitar one night and Pierce being enthralled by a tune I played and had learned when I was a teenager, sung by Nina and Frederick, a Scandinavian couple with haunting voices: "Oh sinner man, where ya gonna run to."

"Sinnerman" ended up as the theme tune for Brosnan's remake of *The Thomas Crown Affair*.

From here, the whole concept of a Grey Owl flick took on a pale resemblance of the real story. After St-Gabriel, we moved into Hull's Ramada Inn, about half an hour's drive to Chelsea, where the crew had built a fictional town called Elk River, complete with a working steam train, a bustling lumber mill, and a Hudson's Bay Company store.

The Ramada wasn't urbane enough for Pierce, so they moved him to the Château Laurier in the capital. In Ottawa the paparazzi relentlessly stalked Brosnan and Galipeau, following them up to the movie set near Chelsea. It was bedlam. Security guards had difficulty holding back scores of stargazers and photographers, while teenage girls begged to work as extras for nothing. One impassioned woman pressed her bare breasts against the window of Brosnan's limo and shouted profane carnal desires, all the while holding on to the hand of her six-year-old daughter. Still, Brosnan never lost his cool.

The village was impressive, expensive to construct, but it had no resemblance to Archie's real world. It was too contrived, too textbook, and way too clean. The Temagami lodge where Grey Owl was to meet Anahareo, Camp Wabikon, was on an island; here, at Elk River, you could be shuttled out to it by courtesy truck. The life scenes of Archie Belaney were put into a compactor and shredded, along with the story. Granted, it was easier to film the various scenes this way, but the village concept had not been thoroughly researched. Like Grey Owl's life, the producers extracted any of the seedier aspects of northern Ontario life. Archie's world had been sanitized.

On the morning they were to shoot the movie's big fight scene, Brosnan paddled out onto the Gatineau River to escape the press, the fans, and the stress of shooting. I followed in another canoe and met up with him. I had about fifteen minutes to teach him the cross-bow draw stroke for the scene coming up. Brosnan was now a confident paddler, though he favoured one side and could not yet turn the canoe in tight corners. He remained stiff-looking, afraid to lean the canoe for fear of tipping in the cold river water.

In the fight scene, after a knife-throwing scrap in the HBC store, Grey Owl is pursued by three angry trappers, all in canoes. Instead of trying to outrun them, he lays his paddle across the gunwales, folds his arms defiantly, and waits. When they arrive, he takes them on and, one by one, they end up in the water while the crowd on the dock cheers.

But there were problems. They filmed a number of takes, some with Brosnan, and some with his stunt double. One scene had to be cut because Brosnan forgot to take off his Ray Bans, and he was getting frustrated. I made my way through the actors, technicians, and grips, and met him by the edge of the newly constructed wharf.

"The wind's come up," I warned him.

"I know," he said. "It's getting tough to keep the canoe still."

I told him I'd have two sandbags put in the front of the canoe to keep the bow from swinging in the gusts. Brosnan nodded, climbed out of the canoe, and took my arm.

"C'mon mate, let's take a look. I want to know what you think."

We walked over to Attenborough and watched the different takes played back on the camera monitor.

"Smooth strokes, Pierce," I told him. "Compensate for the wind by applying just a little more pry after each stroke."

There was an annoying and persistent tap on my back between the shoulder blades:

"*Your hero is doing the goon-stroke, shaganash.*"

It was Archie. He was dressed as one of the bit-part actors, braids tucked under a large canvas hat. He was right. Brosnan's stunt double was a goon-stroker, paddling with an improper J-stroke often used by neophytes to steer a canoe. "*It'll show,*" Archie added.

I talked with the stunt man, who told me that he couldn't do the proper stroke because he had shattered most of the bones in his right arm.

"That won't do," Brosnan said. "I'll do the stunts myself."

He walked over to the canoe, climbed back in, and paddled away.

"*What do you think, Owl, do you approve? He looks better than you,*" I said to Archie.

Archie just shrugged his shoulders. "*This should be amusing,*" he said.

Two divers in wetsuits were conscripted to help Brosnan out with the canoe spins. A rope was attached to each end of the canoe and the divers submerged holding on to the rope. The bad guys approached (all goon-strokers), and Brosnan Owl had to spin the canoe. The divers tugged too hard and almost spilled Brosnan out of the canoe into the frigid water. After a couple of more tries, the turn looked impressive but unnatural. The fight scene was horrible, unlikely, lacked the 007 quick-fire movements to make it remotely exciting, and had cost the producers a million dollars to shoot.

"*I can't watch this,*" Archie said. He walked away disgusted.

The last night of the Chelsea shoot, Brosnan and I and a few of the crew gathered at the bar of the Château Laurier to have a Guinness or two. My job as personal trainer was finished, unless they actually needed me to run the rapids for the opening scene. I had designed a prototype canoe, on paper only, replete with hidden flotation bags and thigh straps, which would effectively replicate Owl's run down the oversized rapids (and make it to the bottom).

Brosnan lamented the fact that he had never learned how to piss out of a canoe.

"The most wonderful gift I shall take away from this film," he admitted, "is the ability to paddle a canoe."

As for me, well, I've got my 007 poster mounted on the wall, inscribed, LOVE ... AND GOOD LIFE — GREY OWL/PIERCE BROSNAN. But my enduring distaste for the movie still resonates, and the realization that Brosnan was merely filling a role for big bucks and no conscience ended our relationship on a sour note.

There were many side effects to this movie. Procuring beaver kits for the shoot was problematic for the producers. They finally found what they wanted from South America, real baby beavers, but had two skinned out and made into puppets. These could be hand-held if the real beavers didn't play their part. Attenborough had coerced Kirk Wipper from the Canadian Canoe Museum to lend Ajawaan Productions some of his personal artifact collection. Attenborough took it upon himself to gift his wife with Kirk's property and the items were never returned.

During a conversation with Pierce in private, I had asked if he would be interested in supporting the fight to save Temagami pine from extinction — something Grey Owl would have done without question. Pierce held up his hands to form the letter *T* and told me in no uncertain terms, "Time out ... I'm a one-issue environmentalist; the whales are my only interest. Anyway, I'm in the process of buying a rainforest logging company. What do you think about that?"

I didn't answer. And I felt that Brosnan only told me this to shut me up, to stop pestering him about being a crusader. Brosnan was an honourable man so long as you had something to offer him. Soon after the movie shoot, and before it was released, I had published a story about the film in a national magazine. The distribution company that bought the Canadian rights to the film put my story on its website. No American company would touch the film — outside of Great Britain and Canada, Grey Owl was virtually an unknown. It wouldn't sell. Brosnan was enraged about my article, even though I painted him as an honourable man but a bad actor. My name was removed from the credits.

The canoe fight scene never saw the light of day. It couldn't be fixed, even with special effects magic. And the first scene was changed, opening with Grey Owl 007 paddling across a serene northern lake, and then changed again to a powwow scene. But he paddled as if he knew what he was doing and that was the important thing. Archie himself might have been pleased. But the movie lacked any pith, any character flaws, or mystery; it was devoid of the drama that defined Grey Owl's true personality. It was evident, perhaps, that Attenborough had lost it as a producer, proving that not all historical characters can be transmogrified into marketable Hollywood icons.

8

RAPID TRANSIT

But there are those amongst us, some who have earned the right to follow their own judgement in such matters; these now take control of the situation. They are the "white water men," to whom the thunderous roar of the rapids and the smell of spray flying in the face are as the intoxication of strong drink.

— Grey Owl, *Men of the Last Frontier*

Running rapids on a wild river in a canoe is entirely a white man thing. Originally, Native Canadians respected their fragile canoes and disdained running fast water for fear of damaging their craft. Early traders and explorers were driven by time and seasonal constraints, and it was deemed more important to tempt fate on the whitewater runs rather than waste time portaging supplies over arduous trails.

Today it's a sport for the adventure seeker. And there are over thirty million whitewater paddlers in North America, few if any are bumping their canoes down boulder strewn rapids in a quest for furs, or pushing westward in search of a location for a new trading post. Aside from the adrenalin rush and the fear of death, there is an actual science to it all — the *knowing*, or the appreciation of the power of water; and more than that there is the acute awareness of the *consequence* of your actions. Good whitewater paddlers have all this down pat, but for the neophyte (and most fit in to this category) there needs to be a Plan B and even a Plan C just in case things don't go down as anticipated. And for these burgeoning enthusiasts the success of the run may be gauged in how well you recovered from your mistakes. Grey Owl, and myself I might add, used the canoe for the work at hand and were put on government salary to tend to the management of forests and parks and beavers. The canoe was to us as the car is to the commuter. Running a rapid could be analogous to a hyper-fast, rush-hour retreat, dodging vehicles along a busy thoroughfare. Grey Owl elaborates on the thrill of the run:

> Rocks that would rip the bottom from a canoe at a touch, lie in wait, invisible, just below the surface, but indications of their position are apparent only to the practised eye. Eddies, that would engulf a pine tree, tug at the frail canoe essaying to drag it into the vortex. Treacherous cross-currents snatch viciously at the paddles; deceptive, smooth-looking, oily stretches break suddenly into six-foot pitches. To such as these considerations of life and limb loom small compared with the maddening thrill of eluding and conquering the frenzied clawing and grasping of tons of hungry, rushing waters; yet coupled with this stern joy of battle is a skill and a professional pride that counts the wetting of a load, or the taking of too much water, an ineradicable disgrace.

THE SOUND

This is a dead giveaway that something is up ahead. The current is picking up noticeably now, quite often before you hear anything. Caution should be the first intonation, especially if you haven't paddled this river before. Avid "whitewaterists" know the nuances of rapid noise in a quick assessment of the pitch — the higher the pitch, the shallower the rapid. The variances can also determine whether the rapid is just a cobblestone riffle or a full-fledged canoe-eating boulder garden or waterfall. It's part of the *knowing*, and takes years of practice. With some voluminous rapids you actually *feel* the sound in the pit of your stomach, and this sparks the neurotransmitters to do their work. There is often no visible warning at all, and if the wind is following your tail, you may not hear anything until you're right on top of it.

THE SCOUT

The standard scouting of a whitewater run entails beaching your canoe at the head of the rapids and walking the portage or following the shore. You then study the layout of the run looking for precipitous drops, ledges, gnarly mid-channel rocks, sweepers (fallen trees that produce a "strainer" with its branches that could be problematic — worse if you run into the tree itself). After this you commit it all to memory. The problem with this method is the fact that nothing looks the same as it did from the shore once you're in the boat moving fifteen kilometres an hour between jagged boulders and yelling at your partner to draw left. The scout works well on short, easy rapids, but for the long runs (I've been on some rapids on Arctic rivers that were more than ten kilometres long), you have to use a different strategy. If you're good at it, you can play the eddies (pools of calm water behind boulders or along the shore), and pick your way down to the bottom with success. Or you can go for broke as I've witnessed many neophytes do, and ricochet from rock to rock like a pinball until you come out at the end, usually bottom side up. No plan, no scout, and no finesse.

POINT BREAK

Once committed to a run and there's no turning back, your body starts to do all kinds of wonderful things. The heart rate increases, pupils dilate, your blood sugar level elevates, and all your senses become crystal clear.

The adrenal glands have just kicked in, releasing a hormone called epinephrine, better known as adrenalin, boosting the supply of oxygen and glucose to the brain and muscles. At the same time, other non-emergency processes (such as digesting the salami and cheese you just had for lunch) is suppressed. It's the "fight-or-flight" response; only this isn't a reaction to something unplanned or necessarily life-threatening, but a premeditated act of bravado.

The 1991 movie *Point Break* popularized the phrase "adrenalin junkie" to describe individuals who thrive on the adrenalin rush of dangerous activities. River junkies, like me, are hooked on the sensual pleasures of riding fast water; so much so that I've heard some whitewater addicts make the claim that shooting a good rapid is better than making love. It does come close, I have to admit, and the activities are strangely similar in that there is the finesse of foreplay, the nitty-gritty of the execution, and the final climax — smoking a cigarette as you rest in the black pool of ecstasy. Partnering with the release of epinephrine are the endorphins — we can thank the pituitary gland for this rush of hormones, all the good things brought on by pain or pleasure, even orgasm. These are the body's natural pain relievers that allow us to feel a sense of control that takes us over the threshold and into the calm eddy below.

So, if we actually are to become good at running whitewater with any level of success and self-adulation (and self-control), it may be to one's advantage to learn the manoeuvres beforehand; perhaps think of the rapid run as making love, to take our time to play the gradations of carnal expectations, hold back, massage the eddies, and wait for the final plunge. For those who blindly thrust their canoes down the middle of the rapid, often prematurely vaulting themselves and their loads into the maelstrom, it can be considered a terrible waste of endorphins.

In 1966 I went on my first one-week canoe expedition on the Mattawa River; two fifteen-year-olds, an old canvas canoe, and the river. It was there that I had my first taste of running fast water. The self-gratification from that initial taste of the maelstrom, of fear and self-made triumph over something bigger than me, irrevocably changed the way I viewed life. Grey Owl's depiction of the river had been carved into my teenage head with a sharp hunting knife:

> Few may know the feeling of savage exultation which possesses a man when the accumulated experience of years, with a split-second decision formed after a momentary glimpse through driven, blinding spume into some seething turmoil, and a perfect coordination between hand and eye, result in, perhaps, the one quick but effective thrust of the paddle or pole, that spells the difference between a successful run, and disaster.

My trips soon became engagements of self-discovery; to test limits and assuage the compulsion to discover what I could do in a canoe. There were times I nearly died in the cold waters after a spill. Life jackets were frowned upon, still, and I couldn't see Archie the intrepid forest provocateur with one strapped around his torso.

In the 1970s few paddlers ever donned life jackets. The word itself was an oxymoron: wearing a kapok-filled, often waterlogged and bulky preserver could have just as easily been the cause of death as tumbling unsheathed down a set of bouldery cascades. If they were mandatory (as they were in the park service or guiding for canoe camps) then they were covertly shoved under the seat or wedged into the stern crevice once you cleared the watchful scrutiny of authority. You engaged only what you were able to safely run, anyway; and because technology lagged in the designing of form-fitting jackets, the preserver was scorned for its discomfort. Techno-gear would replace, in an entirely obtuse way, the need for skill and circumspection — your pliable, indestructible canoe of Royalex, personal flotation device, and float-jacket will suffice.

The art of waterproofing gear had not been perfected either; a sudden dump could result in sodden camping gear and food if the extrication was difficult and long. Today gear is packed in hard-plastic barrels, impervious to water and wildlife, or in waterproof seal-bags. A dump in the rapids is no longer a big deal ... unless. Rivermen in Archie's time often lost their lives log-driving or in a canoe on whitewater, none of whom had any safety gear with them other than their wits. Often poor or indifferent swimmers, death would overtake the man in short order, swept under a log-jam, pinned below the surface in a cauldron or boil, but the cause never attributed to anything but bad luck.

Years later I read Grey Owl's accounts of running whitewater and realize that he probably seldom ran his canoe over anything as spectacular as a wily Class II rapid in spring flood. His favourite river, the Mississauga, like most Shield rivers below the Height of Land, conformed to the typical pool-and-drop geo-fluvial layout — short, fast rapids ending in large pools or small lakes. Not to play down his abilities; some of the most difficult and technical runs are located here. But the finesse demanded by the grand rivers of the boreal and Arctic landscapes far exceeds the old-fashioned skills employed in the time of the canoe brigades. Rapids far too long to scout, with rollers the size of school buses and water running frigid and fast demand both a stalwart and fearless perspective. Archie didn't have to worry about barren ground grizzly bears, man-hunting polar bears, incessant winds with no cover, and a lack of firewood to cook his food. Today his skills would be considered mediocre. It doesn't make him less of a champion.

9

OF MICE AND MEN

They are of all shapes and sizes, these shy, elusive Dwellers among the Leaves who have broken the rules of all the furtive folk, and have come from out the dark circle of the woods to stay with me, some permanently and others from time to time. They range all the way from the small, black, woolly beaver-mouse who goes hopefully around wondering when I am going to leave the lid off the butter-dish …
— Grey Owl, *All Things Both Great and Small,*
"Tales of an Empty Cabin"

It is the non-life-threatening things that can strip a man of his dignity in the wilds. You spend enough time in the out of doors and particular accents are assigned to the things that affect your sanctity of life in order of comfort, or fear, or necessity; and it isn't necessarily the most dangerous threats that bring an adventurer to his knees. Weather can be mediated by shelter and heat; bears can be dealt with by remedial measures. But if you live by simple means in the country, perhaps in an old cabin or homestead, or by chance come across a trapper's cabin while canoeing, you will have come into contact with mice.

To most people, mice are inconsequential rodents that periodically invade their lives in a minor way at the cottage or at the home of a

country relative, and we pay little attention to them. And, while I consider myself to be a conservationist, I have succumbed to primitive urges to hunt and trap in the past, but never for sport or recreation. I live in the midst of a veritable cornucopia of wild creatures, most of whom are welcome guests to the land that's been assigned to me. But mice are never welcome, however cute with their tiny black eyes, big ears, and anthropomorphized history. I hate them with a particular and well-founded zeal, and I kill them with lethal efficiency. It's more than just waking up in the morning to find a dollop of mouse crap on my toothbrush; these creatures are the foulest beasts on the face of the earth, despoiling everything they come into contact with.

We had mice at our cottage when I was a kid, and it was often my job to dispose of the dead, trapped mice outside. The women in my family, except my grandmother, who could eviscerate fish into tidy little fillets, were all squeamish when it came to even seeing a dead mouse — the live ones scurrying beneath the dining room table legs and chairs could wreak havoc and have the room in total mayhem while my granny wielded the broom with insane accuracy. It was always a momentous occasion when in the morning, set traps from the night before yielded the "catch of the day" — tiny bodies crushed, mouths still welded to the morsel of cheese, and six-year-olds vying to be the one to dispose of the dead.

Mice are a necessary component in the natural world. They breed and multiply faster than any other species and provide tasty snacks for a multitude of predators, from owls to wolves. All members of the rodent family — shrews, voles, and mice — have voracious appetites and will eat just about anything to stay alive and do what they do best: propagate.

To this end, it is no wonder that many a remote cabin is infested with mice that seek refuge from predators and a ready supply of food nearby. Sad it is, for those weary travellers, trappers, and prospectors who collapse into their bunks after a hard day, to try and sleep whilst a company of mice scrabble about unwashed dishes and scurry about chattering in their squeaky voices throughout the long night, getting in to all sorts of mischief.

During my early travels by canoe and snowshoe I have chanced upon many a cabin and taken refuge there, either because of weather, fatigue, or curiosity. Some cabins are left in immaculate shape, doors unlocked as it is the code of the North to do so, and shelves stocked with provisions, bunks neat and clean, and a corn-broom left conspicuously in the corner. This is certainly not the norm. The majority of wilderness shacks are in various stages of decomposition and neglect: roofs leaking, log walls un-chinked, mouldy mattresses sporting a mosaic of stains and human detritus; yet, they hold enough trappings of food to encourage the proliferation of mice … food bits on the floor are the first to go, then whatever is left on the shelves or counters in packages and bins, even a bar of soap by the sink will have been whittled away. Once the food source disappears, though, mice can get nasty. The first time I was attacked by deer mice it took me a while to figure out what was happening.

I was canoeing with an old friend when the weather turned sour several days out on an early spring trip, rain turning to snow with a chilling wind out of the north. A log cabin appeared just at the time we were looking for a campsite to pitch our tents, and the decision was made to set up camp in the shack instead of fighting the elements and sleeping on the sodden ground. This was our first mistake. The lure of substantial shelter, along with other amenities, such as a wood stove and the promise of comforting heat, obfuscated the somewhat "minor" annoyances.

Old cabins have a particular aroma, the level and intensity of which depends on the state of care, or rather *un*care. Owners of these domiciles have either departed this earth, gotten too old to do the repairs, or have little time or money to devote to maintenance. And as with anything organic in Nature, left alone in the elements it will biodegrade over time; once the roof starts to leak, the dampness acts like a cancer, rot blossoming incrementally until all that's left are the nails and door hinges, shards of glass from windows, the rusted stove — most of which will also eventually disappear, except perhaps for the modern plastics and glass bottles strewn about the place uncaringly. And so, as time takes hold of these decrepit sanctuaries, there erupts the smell of age, of mildew and rot, a particular musk emanating up from the floorboards from snake nests and perhaps a groundhog or even a skunk. But most of all there is the smell of mice and their industry.

"*This place is pretty run down,*" I said to Archie. He didn't answer. Instead he busied himself unloading the canoe, humming something, happy as if he'd just come home from a long trip. The door was stuck shut, swelled from the rain, a little skewed as the cabin had settled comfortably into the ground. Once inside, we were immediately greeted with an overpowering stench of rot, mouse shit, and bat guano.

"Christ, Owl, I can't believe you actually lived in here!"

"Don't go shaganash on me," Owl retorted, flipping mouldy mattresses over to reveal a moderately cleaner side of filth. It was his way of getting rid of the collected animal feces off the beds, like turning your underwear inside out and putting it back on.

Old, mummified beaver castor hung from the rafters; a pair of unusable snowshoes with worn-through babiche found a place amongst scads of animal stretcher-frames piled in one corner. There was a kitchen counter, of sorts, decorated haphazardly with an array of blackened pots and steel fry pans, cleaned long ago of food bits by hungry mice, and any dish left right-side up was coated with the little tell-tale "cigar-shaped" droppings of cabin mice. On a wall shelf there was a lineup of mostly empty bottles of scotch — the ones without caps held a bottom treasure of dead mice that had now become a fetid soup of barely recognizable critters. Trapped in such places, mice will eventually eat each other to death, the resulting smell attracting yet more mice. And there is always a steady flow of them until all-out war is raged by the cabin owner, or, in his absence, a marten moves into the vicinity or the food source thins out and the population dwindles.

The smell of decay in our particular cabin was thick enough to make you wonder what manner of particulate passed through your lungs at every breath. *"You'll get used to it,"* Archie assured me as he stirred old dead coals in the wood stove with a poker, crumpled up an old sugar bag and threw that and a handful of kindling inside, struck a match on the side of the stove and in the span of about fifteen seconds had a fire going. Owl moved with swift deftness within the confines of familiarity, emptying packs, setting out his bedroll, lighting the oil lamp on the table, each hand occupied at doing something different.

"You're a multi-tasker, Owl, you know that?" I said.

"A what?"

"A multi-tasker … someone good at doing several things at once."

"*You mean someone who can do several things at once well,*" Archie retorted.

"*Whatever.*"

The heat from the wood stove accentuated even more the stench of the place. It was hard to think about making dinner. It would be a quick, one-pot meal; no dicing and chopping of garlic and herbs as usual tonight. Owl had strung his wet oilskins over a rafter directly above the stove, adding his own brand of aroma to the already full elixir of olfactory malodour. We ate in silence.

"*Not your usual epicurean delight tonight, Wilson,*" Archie lamented as he forked the last morsel into his mouth, pulled a hanky from his back pocket, and daintily swiped his face clean.

"*Owl, you should be used to bully-beef and rice,*" I said. Plates were left on the counter and forgotten while Archie went into a long diatribe about war rations and how sick he was of canned corned beef.

The heated cabin awoke an infinite number of wild folk within, the feeble light of the lantern catching fragments of movement; spiders dropping from the ceiling on spindles of web; wood roaches scurrying through and over wet floorboards, moving faster than your ability to crush them underfoot; a bat fluttered by Owl's head and, without getting out of his chair, he kicked the door open to let it out; something stirred under the cabin, knocking against a floor joist, followed by a steady grinding, gnawing sound. But it was the mice that caught my immediate attention. They were everywhere … lots of them … countless legions of them.

Finding an old mouse trap, I covered the catch with peanut butter and set the trap on the counter and waited. Archie sat there grinning, smoking his pipe. I watched as mouse after deer mouse licked the catch clean of peanut butter without setting off the trap even once. That having failed to reduce the population, I filled a deep bowl with multi-hook fishing lures, each hook sporting a dollop of peanut butter. Feeling smug with my new invention — *the better mouse trap* — I felt comfortable enough to crawl in to my sleeping bag for the night. Sleep did not come easily.

Not having washed the plates of food, they were left with their dirty cutlery on the counter, along with the baited bowl of hooks. As a light sleeper, any noise out of the ordinary will keep me awake. And so, as an orchestra tunes in that pre-concert, grating cacophony, mice will go to great lengths to produce similar annoying noise amongst forks and spoons and cups and left-out food packages and, curiously enough, a bowl of deadly, mouse-catching fish hooks. I could hear them rattling around in the bowl; rapalas, flatfish, bobbers, and jigs, hooks piercing the soft fleshy mouths of demon mice. After listening for some time, the rattling in the bowl eventually ceased and curiosity demanded a quick look by flashlight to see the carnage I had inflicted with my mouse trap. To my surprise, the fishing lures were all still in the bowl, each hook licked clean of peanut butter. Archie let out a big sigh and rolled over in his wool blanket.

"*Shaganash,*" he moaned under his breath.

Frustrated but not defeated, I found a hole in the back wall where the mice seemed to be coming in and I stood there with an axe in one hand and a flashlight in the other waiting for the first one to pop though.

Whack! "*Shit ... little bugger's are quick!*"

Whack! Another miss. *Whack!* "*Dammit, Archie do something!*"

"*No,*" Archie said.

"*Why not, you're supposed to be an expert in these things.*" I took aim again and missed, but took a big chip off the corner of the bunk above Archie's head.

"*I'm having too much fun watching you carrying on like some crazed banshee.*" Archie laughed.

I had one last option ... *the gun!* On fall canoe trips it wasn't unusual to take along a 410 shotgun or .22 calibre rifle for partridge hunting. I had a scope mounted on my .22 for target shooting and I was a fair shot at seventy-five metres. Hunting mice at close range could be tricky. I loaded up the old spring-loaded mousetrap with peanut butter and set it near the door — another place where the mice were getting in. Lying on my belly in the furthest corner from the trap (which was only about five metres away), I sighted the gun on the set trap and waited. It wasn't long before a mouse arrived and began licking the PB off the catch.

Bang!

"*What the blazes!*" Archie yelled, hitting his head on the upper bunk as he tried to get to his feet, hand groping for his sheath knife.

"*Archie, look, I got em,*" I cried.

"*No you didn't. You shot the catch off the trap and the trap caught him. There's no mark on the mouse except a broke neck.*"

Sure enough, I couldn't get a proper sighting on the mouse, shooting low and setting off the trap. That wasn't all I shot.

"*Look here, Daniel Boone, you shot a hole through the door and killed two life jackets and a paddle.*"

I fell asleep out of sheer exhaustion. Some days on the trail can be gruelling, and mice or no mice, I was going to get some sleep. I don't know if it was in my dream or not, but there was a chewing sensation on my finger just above the first joint, and I let it go on for some time. It persisted, only intensifying until it actually started hurting and I knew it wasn't a dream.

"*Christ … the damn mouse was eating my finger!*" I brought my other fist down on the side of the bunk, hoping to connect with my attacker, but he was already gone. For the next hour or so I kept up a steady vigil of flicking mice off my bed, listening to them as they landed several feet away and scurried off into some dark corner. I nodded off, for how long I don't know, but I woke up with a mouse clinging onto my earlobe.

"*Sheeeeittt!*"

"*Enough!*" yelled Archie. "*Now I can't sleep! I'll show you how to catch mice. Then we can both get some rest.*" Archie almost beamed, as if he were waiting for this moment just to show me up.

Owl went out the back of the cabin with the lantern. He refused to use the flashlight. I told him to be careful not to walk in circles, trapped in the narrow beam of light cast by the oil lantern, and get himself lost. He laughed. He came back in with a five-gallon steel pail, lid missing, and laid it on its side on the cabin floor. Taking a hammer and nail, he punched two holes at opposite ends near the top opening. He lit the stove again and put the coffee pot on to boil.

"*Want some coffee, shaganash?*" Owl crooned.

"*Why not. Neither of us is getting any sleep tonight anyway.*"

Archie poured the remainder of the Carnation milk into our cups, then punched a hole in the middle of each end of the can with a nail.

He then took a coat hanger and straightened it out, first pushing an end through one side of the pail, then skewering the milk can, and finally passing the stiff wire through the opposite end of the pail. The milk can revolved smoothly on the wire. Shuffling through the food pack, he pulled out the peanut butter and set it on the table. He took his sheath knife and scooped enough PB to smear around the entire middle of the milk can. Grabbing a pot, he marched outside and went down to retrieve water from the lake. The water was then poured into the pail to a depth of about four inches. The contraption[5] was pushed beside the woodpile and Owl fashioned a ramp up to the trap wire with a flat piece of cedar kindling. He turned down the light to a candle glow, pushed his chair against the back wall, and put his stockinged feet up on the table.

"This'll be more fun than watching one of my National Film Board documentaries," Owl commented, waiting for my response patiently.

"I couldn't agree with you more, Owl, although I have to admit … I never actually saw any of your movies in their entirety. I found your voice to be a bit irritating."

"How do you mean?" Owl queried, a little on edge.

"Well, your voice doesn't suit your demeanour. It's a bit squeaky, you know, not really what you would expect for such a rugged guy."

"Hey, look — they're here," Archie barked.

And they were. Two line-ups of mice fought to get on the wire and jump to the PB-laden milk can. And one after the other they rolled off the rotating can and into the water at the bottom of the pail, swimming aimlessly for about five minutes before giving up. Mice float. And eventually a raft of dead mice appears whereupon some of the fallen take

---

5   I was actually shown how to make this perpetual mousetrap by the late Gordon Guppy, descendent of Bill Guppy — the "King of the Woodsmen" — whom Archie Belaney stayed with when he first arrived in Temagami in 1907. Of course, Archie would have gravitated to this "colourful" character right off and was lucky to be taken in and taught many of his outdoor skills by Bill, including throwing knives for the tourists. Temagami was famous for its "dollar bill" tricks. This one worked well for Archie: a tourist would pin a dollar bill against a tree, and if he could throw a knife and cut it in half, the dollar was his. Since American tourists were gullible (and somewhat fearful of "Red Indians"), local Anishnabai would come to the bars and ask the tourists if they would like to see the dollar trick. The player would collect dollar bills from around the table, then walk smartly to the bar and buy himself a drink, leaving the tourists a little dumbfounded.

refuge for a short time, but they die, too, after a while. We stopped counting after thirty-eight mice and returned triumphantly to our bedrolls, the tinny sound of a milk can spinning about every two minutes, and the gasping puffs and grunts of those doomed to drown at the bottom of a steel pail filtering though the cabin as a sweet lullaby. I slept.

Mice have this propensity to nest just about anywhere, as if the mother mouse forgot she was pregnant and about to give birth and suddenly realized she forgot to find a place to have them. And it is quite unfathomable as to the speed in which they can construct a nest of certain elaborate proportion. This happened to me on several occasions while canoeing in the North: having set up camp in the evening, and leaning a canvas gear pack against a tree, the top flap having been securely cinched down with leather straps, it was left for the night. In bear country, pots and pans would be stationed on top of the pack(s) as a deterrent,[6] the larger animals obviously more clumsy than mice, and mice have a peculiar way of getting into the smallest of orifices without making a sound. Once having risen and completed the morning rituals, I set about packing up my gear. As I opened the flap of my gear pack, out jumped two white-footed mice; they promptly ran up my arm and catapulted off the back of my neck. Reaching into the bottom of the pack, I felt a sizable ball of tree bark and moss, which I pulled out and examined. Curled inside were several pink-skinned and squirming baby mice, eyelids pulled tight over their soon-to-be inquisitive black eyes. Even with a patent distaste for mice, I couldn't bring myself to kill them, which I could have easily done by throwing them in the still smouldering campfire, or tossing them in to the river; instead, I tucked the nest into a hollow log near the pack in hopes that the parent mice would smell their babies and return to the nest.

While homesteading on the Ottawa River, north of the village of Mattawa, my cabin was often invaded by mice, particularly in the late

---

6   Out of the many hundreds of camp nights I've spent in the bush, I've only ever slung my packs from trees as a bear deterrent on two occasions. All other nights I would simply pile pots and pans on top of kitchen packs and wannigan as an "early-warning" alarm — bears, skunks, raccoons, et cetera, would knock the pots down, the resultant noise usually being enough to make them hightail it into the woods. If this failed, I would then have to get up and chase them off.

fall. It was all-out war, and at times I felt that I was fighting against uneven odds. Having arrived at the local dump in my jeep one morning, I noticed smoke coming from the engine. Lifting the hood with some dread I was greeted by a waft of smoke which included the recognizable smell of cooked meat. Once the smoke cleared, I noticed a straw nest tucked into the manifold, which by this time had mostly burned off, leaving behind the blackened bodies of baby mice.

Mice will go to any lengths to get inside. I had installed a small propane fridge in my kitchen, the back of which was vented to the outside so that it was flush with the inside wall of my kitchen. In the winter the propane was shut off, as the contents would naturally stay cool. For several days we had been using the bagged milk, the type you snip a half-inch corner off the bag, the bag sitting snugly in a plastic container. After about four days I noticed an "off" taste to the milk; not the usual unpleasant sour taste, but more … earthy. Holding the bag up to the light I noticed there was something floating at the bottom of the bag. Draining out the milk revealed a bloated dead mouse which upon closer inspection of the dumped milk also included a few popped turds. The gag reflex that followed was founded upon the fact that we had been ingesting the foul effluent of this critter for several days, albeit mostly in our morning coffee, nonetheless affecting the taste enough to assure that it was something other than the brand of java.

How did they get in the fridge?

A close inspection outside revealed a small slit of space in the door of the enclosed box I had built around the fridge; from there the mouse had chewed a hole through three-inches of Styrofoam and foil backing to gain access to the contents of the fridge.

Aside from the fact that mice can violate anything they come into contact with by crapping on counters, tables, dishes, and on top of the toothbrush left at the side of the bathroom sink, mice are notorious for other deeds equally foreboding. In less than a night, if given the opportunity to discover unprotected bags of rice, seeds, nuts, or grains, one mouse can move two pounds of it clear across the cabin to be stored in between the clothes in the third drawer of the bedroom dresser, packed in the toe of a boot, or even under the covers at the end of an unoccupied bed.

The ritual of opening up my wilderness cabin generally happens in May, as soon as the ice is off. Having set up my mouse barrel trap the previous November (using a five-gallon plastic restaurant pail, a coat hanger, and a Carnation milk tin) it would have been sitting for almost six months without being dumped out. To keep the water at the bottom of the pail from freezing, it's customary to add antifreeze or gasoline to the mix; it also helps break down the organic matter.

Upon arriving at the cabin and opening the door you are immediately greeted with the aroma of a successful winter catch; layer upon layer of mice having "cooked" in the spring heat are now liquefied. Unfortunately, there is nothing you can really do to mask the stench. The trap is dumped in the bush and reset.

Sometimes the trap will be set up in the "guest" cabin, which is open to all canoeists who stop by for shelter during foul weather. Guests often include young teenagers from canoe camps who kindly sign the guest journal upon leaving. Although most visitors are appreciative of the hospitality bestowed upon them, and they make a point of saying so in the camp logbook, those confronted by the "loaded" mouse barrel almost always leave disparaging remarks and wonder at the level of cruelty I inflict upon such tiny, helpless forest creatures.

In "Tales of an Empty Cabin," Grey Owl writes, "People having the dim, distorted ideas that are held by so many concerning animals, can gain very little insight into their true natures. Each animal has his separate personality, easily distinguishable to one who knows him."

PART TWO

LANDSCAPES

There is a common myth that is shared, agreed upon, and circulated by certain members of the canoeing elite. Emanating from the critical ranks of academia, professors, for the most part, tend to trivialize and often demean landscapes within the "near" wilderness as having few remaining attractive qualities, that true adventure and experiences can only be had in the Arctic or lower boreal regions. Granted, most intrusive resource extraction takes place within the accessible, forested regions of the country — a visible desecration by capitalist aggressors — but there are landscapes preserved in their primitive state within close proximity to over-tended parks, outer suburbia, and cottage country. One can get lost or perish within a short hike from a busy road as easily as they can five hundred kilometres from the nearest northern community.

Wilderness and landscapes are entwined within an indefinable, almost cosmic realization of self, and a higher consciousness of our place in the greater picture. Roads, parks, industrial or commercial developments may not have altered a nearby "wild" landscape in the least, as is the case with many famous geographical destinations. One can have a pure sense of aloneness and have the capacity to indulge in a "wilderness" experience a short walk from their vehicle on a country road.

Henry David Thoreau wrote in his journal, August 30, 1856, that "It is in vain to dream of a wildness distant from ourselves. There is

none such. It is the bog of the brains and bowels, the primitive vigor of Nature in us, that inspires that dream. I shall never find in the wilds of Labrador any greater wildness than in some recess of Concord, i.e. than I import into it."

10

TUNDRA

In places the forest dwindles down to small trees which, giving way to moss and sagebrush thin out and eventually disappear altogether, and the country opens out into one of those immense muskegs or swamps which make overland travel in whole sections of this territory impossible in the summer time. These consist mostly of stretches composed of deep, thin mud, covered with slushy moss and perhaps sparsely dotted with stunted, twisted trees.
— Grey Owl, *Men of the Last Frontier,*
"The Land of Shadows"

Some who are experienced travellers and have lived in the North for some time look down upon the novice visitor to the tundra; they say in a very pompous statement that "those who come to the Arctic once, return and write a book about it; those who come several times end up living here …"

A brash assessment of the neophyte, true to some accounts, but the accurate value of the experience is one's ability to "see" and retain the details of the landscape, the environment, and the resident cultures; it has nothing or little to do with time. Just ask Farley Mowat. True, many modern adventurers go to the Arctic for self-serving, albeit brief, stints, but I know of those ardent explorers who travel for the sake of the journey and are able to absorb all the nuances of the trail in short order.

Fifteen years ago I made my first trip to the tundra. Up until that time I was safely planted within the confines of the forested regions of Canada, not far from access and egress points, manicured parks, and Tim Hortons donut shops. Selling the idea of a Canadian adventure trip to *Men's Journal* magazine — the same publisher that produces *Rolling Stone* out of downtown Manhattan — was a shot in the dark. But they bought the idea and paid me dearly to guide a writer and photographer down Manitoba's Seal River. The Seal was chosen for its Dene history and the fact that it crossed three major biomes — the typical rock country of the boreal Shield, the transitional Land of Little Sticks and treeline region, and the subarctic tundra. Aside from all the other associated events that I have previously written about, including Manitoba's worst boreal wildfires, the Seal adventure earmarked an incredible introduction to a new and profoundly different landscape.

The word *tundra* comes from an obscure Kildin Sami or Lappish dialect (northern Russia), from the word *tundar*, meaning "uplands and treeless mountain tract." The Arctic tundra is a biome where the tree growth is deterred by low temperatures and a short growing season, or, basically, a treeless plain. In Canada it refers to the region where the subsoil is permanently frozen as "permafrost" and the ground cover is predominantly moss, heath grasses, and lichens. Winters are cold and dark, reaching temperatures of minus sixty degrees, but oddly enough, not as bitter cold as it gets in the more southerly boreal forests. In terms of precipitation, the tundra is desert-like, accumulating most of its moisture during the short summer. The permafrost melts just enough to allow plants to grow; the water can't really go anywhere, so it sits on top of the tundra flats as huge bogs, marsh, and quickly draining streams. The low biodiversity of the tundra, however, creates a living environment for an impressive wildlife population: caribou, muskox, tundra wolves, Arctic fox, Arctic hare, lemmings, snowy owl, ptarmigan, and even polar bear thrive at the world's edge.

Most notable is the wind that is an ever-present feature of the tundra. Before I had embarked on the Seal River, an associate guide from Temagami had led an expedition to the Territories that subsequently changed his life. Accompanied by several clients, the two-week river trip had been seriously lengthened to four because of the high winds and inability to traverse any of the large lakes en route. The wind was so powerful, it had blown one of the heavy cedar-canvas boats into oblivion; food ran out and they were forced to kill a caribou to sustain themselves. This, obviously, predated GPS or satellite phone capability and the Type-A businessmen were hot to sue the guide and his company. It's no surprise that the company soon dissolved after the incident. The resolute character of the wind is well-known amongst seasoned Arctic travellers; it can be a blessing as a tailwind or a potentially lethal climax to a badly planned and executed trip. The wind, regardless of its tenacity, seldom seems to work its magic to dispel biting flies.

Seal River Journal, August 12, 1994

Although the tamarack and spruce followed the hem of the Seal, we could see the tundra heath backdrop more regularly. As of yet, we hadn't the opportunity to explore the open tundra. Whereas the park-like manifestation found throughout the spruce lands afforded such a confusing picture of growth and a restricted view of the environs, the open heath would offer a true visage of the Barren Lands persona. The actual phantom "tree-line" took two days and almost one hundred kilometres to traverse. Halfway through the first day since the inferno, we were now officially within the Arctic tundra.

At the bottom of a long and tedious, rock-littered rapid we beached the canoes alongside a rather odd-looking island; large and flat-topped, it stood high above the river course, barren, intriguing, and somewhat formidable. It felt wonderful to stretch the cramped leg muscles and peel off the tops of our wet suits as we climbed the steep, crumbling bank to the apogee of the island. The top surface was uniform, almost unnatural, spongy to walk on and covered with a lush carpet of reindeer lichen. We were standing on a raised peat-plateau, several metres in depth. The view afforded our first unrestricted look at the tundra; and even though we couldn't see much of the river ahead as it sliced its way through the deep tundra mat, the overwhelming nature of the open terrain impressed the senses immensely. We all felt like running, like children at a playground who had been penned-up in a car or house too long. And even with the brisk wind, the black flies continued their onslaught in persistent waves.

Groves of stunted spruce, thick at the bottom stock, gnarled and persecuted by the wind into bowed stature, oftentimes follow down the tundra river valleys, such as the Thelon or the Coppermine, northward away from the boreal sheath. The veneer of trees obscuring a paddler's view of the tundra is actually progressing deeper into the Arctic as the climate changes. The warming trend has prompted animal species such as moose to venture further north, and out of their typical regions. The tundra holds one-third of the world's soil-based carbon within its frozen landscape. With the permafrost melting deeper each season, the release of greenhouse gas is a huge concern. The high banks of a tundra river now bleeds away moisture in visible rivulets during the lengthening summers; inland glaciers once prevalent along the Coppermine River have now totally disappeared. Even a view from the summit of the Coppermine Mountains proved fruitless in our search for the famous tundra glaciers.

The trip down the Seal during the pre-techno-age of wilderness exploring was an enlightening event for me in the way I did things. The method in which you interpret weather and distance and wind and hours of daylight until dark required fine tuning. Headwater lakes of some of the major river systems in the tundra are often choked with ice in early July. The actual window of optimal travel time is quite brief. Larger rivers have dependable water levels but they empty quickly and become veritable rock gardens; smaller rivulets and creeks can disappear completely. Along the coast of Hudson Bay, river estuaries are still under the influence of isostatic rebound — a gradual uplifting caused by the melting of the heavy ice-age glacier covering. This creates a myriad of braided channels and confusing flow patterns that can screw up your choice of outflow direction.

Wind can persist for days. It can wear on your nerves. It makes it impossible to travel, to paddle or portage. Tents are difficult to maintain. It can delay or cancel flights. It can ruin friendships and crash morale. Wind can be your nemesis. But the enemy isn't the wind — it's the inability to stay still and do nothing. The impulsion is to keep moving.

I've probably spent more time hiking the tundra than paddling its rivers, often held up waiting for the wind to subside; to really be aware of the landscape it requires getting some distance from the environment of the river. Often, the two are disparately different in character, and it may take a climb up a ridge-top to get a proper overview of the land. The tundra is seldom flat, as one may think, and is dominated by a rolling, undulating plain, broken by Precambrian rock outcrops and the ubiquitous tundra heath.

I've chanced upon ancient stone circles, grave sites, food caches, Inukshuk and dolmen stones, wolf dens, herds of muskox, pingos, and herds of caribou, only because I took the time to hike away from the river. Following sand eskers, some a hundred metres in height, such as those found along the Thlewiaza, are so alluring that you follow with no regard for the time. And in the tundra, night is but a casual wink of the sun.

Some see the northern tundra as a desolate, depressing place; a grey-sky and white-rock drab world compared with the visually bright and busy landscape to the south. Admittedly, you do feel more insignificant and vulnerable in the Barrens, but at the same time empowered and liberated. Tundra is about time standing still and the never-ending sunset; tundra is a barren ground grizzly sleeping on top of a muskox carcass in the middle of the Coppermine River; tundra is finding enough driftwood for a fire to cook fresh-caught Arctic char and grayling.

Grey Owl talks eloquently of the rivermen who plied the waters of the Land of Shadows, of their stalwart demeanour, energy, and skill in the woods. But what of those individuals who travelled in one of the world's most unwelcoming and often perilous landscapes, like surveyor

J.B. Tyrrell, or even John Hornby, who died of starvation on the banks of the Thelon.

Grey Owl's landscapes were singular in nature, his adaptation to outdoor life almost limited to just over two decades. Some relic outdoorsmen would question whether or not twenty years is enough time to be relegated such high esteem and honour as Grey Owl was bestowed for his wilderness prowess. Today his skills would be challenged easily but his knowledge and ability to convey the heart and soul of the wilderness in words — untouchable.

11

CANADIAN SHIELD

This hinterland yet remains a virgin wilderness lying spread
out over half a continent; a dark, forbidding panorama of
continuous forest, with here and there a glistening lake set
like a splash of quicksilver amongst the tumbled hills.

— Grey Owl

Anyone who has discovered Grey Owl's book *Men of the Last Frontier*
will recognize the place as the "Land of Shadows," that unfathomable
wilderness that defines almost half of Canada's physical landscape. It is
a mysterious frontier "lying just beyond the road and rail," laments Grey
Owl. "It forms a line of demarcation between the prosaic realities of a
land of everyday affairs and the enchantment of a realm of high adventure, unconquered, almost unknown, and unpeopled except by a few
scattered bands of Indians and wandering trappers."

Well, Archie, things have changed somewhat since you plied your
paddle through the crystalline waters of northern Ontario in the 1920s,
but the Land of Shadows continues to cast its spell on those ardent adventurers seeking refuge from urban banality. We know this safehold as the
Canadian Shield, sometimes referred to as the Precambrian or Laurentian
Shield or, in mystical reverence, as the bony carapace of the turtle's back.

It is the oldest place on this planet; four billion years old to be somewhat precise, with one of the world's most stable foundations of igneous

and metamorphic rock, blended through countless geological events. It has evolved into one of the most acclaimed, accessible wilderness landscapes in the world.

"Thus it has lain since the world was young, enveloped in a mystery beyond understanding, and immersed in silence, absolute, unbroken, and all-embracing ..."

Eloquent prose from a man who knew how to translate the way of the trail into story and narrative, capturing the attention of the world, inspiring the masses to turn an eye toward conservation. The Canadian Shield, if nothing more, has presented the stage on which to pursue adventure since time immemorial. It certainly proved so for a European-born, quasi-Indian like Grey Owl, whose capricious wanderings across the northern solitudes resulted in a kick-start to the Canadian environmental movement.

As for me, growing up in a woodlot in rural southern Ontario, I was enamoured by such enchanting sagas of adventure and romance in the Temagami pinelands. At every opportunity I would head north, beyond the pastoral hills and shade trees, mowed lawns and cow pastures, to that amorphous, chaotic mosaic of ancient Indian trails, spirited rivers, and lofty forests.

If I were to reminisce about the Canadian Shield hinterland, reflect upon the last thirty-five years of my life as a guide, outfitter, and homesteader, simple metaphors could only betray the meaning of these poignant experiences. "Go see for yourself," I'd tell people. "Go and stand beside a three-hundred-year-old pine tree, touch the course bark, and hear the earth speak. Hike to the top of a trail-less ridge, once a vision-questing site for Anishnabai youths. Sit, dream, and find your own totem spirit, or ride the back of a wild rapid and embrace the serpentine. Bow to the Master of all things as you gaze upon a granite wall illuminated with the ochre-red artistry of a Native shaman. You had better leave tobacco here or suffer the consequences!"

The personality of the Shield — the shape and texture of the ragged hills, the contour of the rivers, the spectrum of living things that dwell among the shadows — are all attributable to glacial provenance. Loose material has been scraped away, base rocks abraded, shallow basins gouged, drainage channels disrupted. What remain are the myriad lakes and rivers, and erratic boulders strewn across the landscape like players on a terrestrial board game.

The Shield marks the height of land where rivers are born, flowing south to the Great Lakes or north to the Arctic Ocean. The familiar "pool and riffle" character of a Shield river adds to the drama of a whitewater canoe adventure. Alternating sequences of rapids and deep, black pools provide both adventure and respite from the adrenalin thrill.

The Torngat Mountains of Labrador stand guard at the eastern coast of Canada, rising over 1,600 metres out of the cold depths of the north Atlantic. Barren and inhospitable, these ramparts of the Shield deflected the first foreign advance of a thousand years ago. The Norse adventurers (to whom I am genealogically connected) found the alpine glacial coast of the New World too formidable, and steered a more southerly course for Newfoundland. Settlement was sporadic and short-lived. Such is the inimical personality of the Shield's outer vanguard; a land inhabited by a resolute and ancient people — the Dene, Innu, and Inuit.

Half a millennium later, Europe sent the likes of Cabot, Champlain, and Cartier to penetrate the dark realm of the New World. It wasn't long before they realized the wealth of resources that could be plucked from the virgin wilderness. Thus began a rivalry over control of the fur trade that would last three hundred years. In 1801, Sir Alexander Mackenzie first mentioned the rugged lineament of the Canadian interior as having "the same dark rocks extending from Lake Winnipeg to Labrador." It was Austrian geologist Edouard Seuss who coined the word *shield*; to him, its gently domed shape resembled that of a warrior's shield. Unbeknownst to Seuss, Hudson Bay actually formed a rather pronounced depression in the great Shield landmass. Had Seuss known this, he may very well have coined the feature the "Canadian Doughnut" instead.

From the midriff of the Hudson Bay boreal morass, the Shield gradually rises outward. To the north and east are the lofty, barren peaks of Ellesmere Island, Baffin Island, and the Labrador coast; to the northwest, the Barren Lands tundra. To the south, a much different personality unfolds: gently rolling topography, pocked with a medley of forests, fens, lakes, and rivers. This is the part of the Shield as most know it ... as Grey

Owl knew it, although it stretches far beyond the treeline domain into Nunavut and Ungava.

Relatively easy access into the frontier lands helped to change the persona of the wilderness at the turn of the last century, from a savage landscape to a veritable tourist mecca. Canoe recreation burgeoned in the late 1800s, spreading north from New England, across the border into lower Quebec and southern Ontario. When the Ontario government pushed the railroad north to Huntsville in 1870 and established Algonquin Park in 1893, Torontonians flocked to the "new" wilderness.

Other interests in the Shield wealth followed on the heels of a steadily declining fur trade, growing at a rapacious rate beyond the watchful eye of prudence and conservation ethics. Below those smooth bedrock ridges lay a bounty of minerals — gold, silver, iron ore, and nickel. Once a gridwork of transportation lines had been established, and rivers were dammed for hydropower, mining flourished. Luckily, provincial and federal parks and reserves were set aside. Even so, the resource-rich Shield would evoke insurmountable land-use disputes between the various factions, still to be solved in the new millennium.

Logging of the magnificent pine trees had already begun along the Ottawa Valley, and Archie Grey Owl was well aware of the way Ontario's precious forests were quickly disappearing:

> As a woman's hair is — or was — her chief adornment, so Canada's crowning glory is her forests, or what remains of them. With her timber gone, the potential wealth of the Dominion would be halved, and her industries cut down by one-third; yet the forest is being daily offered up for a burnt sacrifice to the false gods of greed and waste, and the birthright of future generations is being squandered by its trustees.

Grey Owl had travelled much of the Ontario and Quebec Shield regions during a huge surge in resource extraction, wanton waste and destruction, not to mention the decline and almost annihilation of the beaver population in Canada. He was legions ahead of his time from an environmental perspective. To move conscious thought toward conservation in such a broad context, today would have earned him a Nobel Environmental Award — in the least, the Order of Canada.

Archie knew the protective armour of the wilderness was flagging under the assault of industry. The Shield could only deflect so many attacks, and he saw, firsthand, the state of diminishing wilderness and aboriginal culture. Profound distinctions in physical temperament and social dynamics regarding land use have always labelled the Canadian Shield as a paradoxical and complex entity. Its untrammelled beauty is incomparable; the ugly truth remains that Grey Owl's hinterland has been pockmarked by clearcut logging, mine effluent, and invasive roads.

If I were to give praise to the persona of the Shield landscape I could display and flaunt thousands of photographs taken over a span of thirty-five years; images from the coast of Labrador, westward across Quebec, Ontario, and Manitoba, and north into the Nunavut Territory. Even with that it would not be sufficient acclaim to elucidate on the merit of the countless sensory attributes — the sound of cascades and falls tumbling over ledges of gneissic or granite rock, or the ghostlike wail of a solitary loon; the fragrant, sweet scent of fallen poplar leaves in the fall; touching the rough, corrugated bark of a white pine tree towering twelve stories above you — that are but a token of the endearments along the trail through the Land of Shadows.

There is a numinous presence surrounding the Shield. Native shamans have left their artistry on the rock faces throughout the Shield territory; pictures on stone using magical elements from the Earth and the spirit world, combined to endure a thousand years of unsympathetic environmental conditions. Mazinaw Rock, Fairy Point, Little Missinaibi Lake, Agawa, Bloodvein, Artery Lake, Tramping Lake to name a very few of the teaching sites with the strange pictographs of animals, people, medicine men, serpents, and canoes. We can only speculate what they mean and the messages hidden within.

To paddle a canoe through a chain of lakes, connected as a contiguous feature of the landscape, quite often following a rift valley, scoured by glaciers, and to trace with your eye the outline of cliff and promontory as you while away your strokes, is hypnotic bliss. The world of the Shield is touchable, personal and intimate, always close and magnanimous. Its physiographic character is unfixed. Weather is forgiving. The water here in the rocky hinterland is lucid and revealing, except in the northern slough of boreal toward Hudson Bay, where the rivers flow murky and wide. There are as many calm days as there are with wind, sunny days to stormy — a co-operative balance for the traveller.

The vegetation is diverse and extreme; from barren east-coast tuka-more — dwarfed bonsai-like conifers thrashed by the salt winds of the Atlantic — to lush Carolinian hardwood forests and ancient pinelands. Leaving the rock knob uplands behind, to the north there is an endless flow of olive green drabness — the boreal lands that eventually give way to the Land of Little Sticks where forests are relegated to mere copses of stunted spruce no bigger around than your wrist, and scattered across a scabrous sun- and fire-scorched topography. And, eventually, the Shield reveals yet another face where trees are as uncommon as people, and the groundcover a variegated master work of art.

But for the most part, the Shield is the place of near adventure, within the shade of the great Canadian forests and the security of cover. Sunsets are short-lived as night descends with clockwork finality; a splash of crimson and orange, the comforting sound of a crackling campfire by the side of a rapid. The wind that tugged at the canoe all day has now settled into a faint memory of the hardship it caused during the day.

The sanctity of a Canadian Shield morning, even for the agnostic, is a divine experience. There is a window of time in which the incident morning light christens lake and forest with its signature wake-up call; wraith-like mists ascending heavenward through the crown of tall pines, mingling with your campfire smoke; spears of golden light, like phosphorous threads, aglow, touching and moving over the wakening landscape in slow progression.

Another moniker depicting the distinctiveness of the Shield is the mosses and liverworts, the variety of which is more pronounced as you approach the Height of Land. Laid distinctly as a carpet over moist hollows, over rotting logs and rocks, anywhere the soil nutrients are deficient; the sphagnum mat is thick and pretentious, abundant more to the mixed conifer forest and the boreal fringe areas. And lichens, too, adorning the rock outcrops in mosaic communities, multi-coloured greys and greens, crisp under the summer sun, moist and pliable after a deluge; the coral and reindeer cladonias, dog-tooth, the goblet-shaped pixie cup lichen are indicative of the richness of life that thrive on dead or decaying or inanimate material and structures in the forest. And, in the latter part of the summer, Indian Pipe pushes its way through the forest detritus in social clusters; an odd herb whose fungal tendrils latch on to the roots of nearby trees. If picked, this "ice plant" seems to melt within the fingers.

Beneath the new growth is an old landscape. There is a resident beauty that comes with age; the fissured bark of the white pine tree, whose young bark is smooth and uninteresting, through time takes on a wizened, sculpted look; even the geologic processes that are constantly breaking down old mountains into tumbled art forms create a landscape that is still evolving.

Grey Owl, in *Men of the Last Frontier,* "Land of Shadows," describes this beauty:

> Not all the wild lands gloom in sullen shadow. There are vistas, unbelievably beautiful, to be seen beyond the boles of giant trees edging some declivity, of sun-drenched valleys, or wide expanse of plain, blue with its luscious carpet of berries. Occasional grassy glades, oases in the sameness of the sunless grottos surrounding them, refresh the mind and eye, seeming intimate and friendly after the aloofness of the stately forest.

12

RIVER WALK

Here and there along its course are mighty waterfalls,
some with rainbows at the foot of them ...
— Grey Owl, *Tales of an Empty Cabin*, "The River"

A river flows one way. From its birth at the headwaters, to its climax in the ocean, the river finds a way through the landscape to its end point. The water journey; the human journey, it's the same. Water is reborn into rain and again delivered to the headwaters; humans are reborn into something else, if you believe in such things. Rivers have personalities, as do people; some placid and demure, others raucous and feral. The water is merely the soul or spirit of the landscape that defines the river; our actions define who we are. A river that has been dammed is like a patient on life-support — the soul is in stasis, its identity uncertain and diminished.

Sometime during my tenure as park ranger in Temagami I had the inclination to study the river most popularized by Grey Owl — the Mississaga River in northern Ontario. I knew little about this river except that it was the main feature in Grey Owl's writings about the trail, of canoemen, and life as a canoe ranger. This was the alluring agent for me and my curiosity, to paddle the river of Grey Owl's notorious fame, to start at Biscotasing Station, and then wend my way down to Aubrey Falls, the spectacular climax of the river as it tumbled recklessly over granite ledges to the dark pools below.

I drove to Aubrey Falls because there was a road to it, as often is the case these days leading to remarkable places in the near wilderness. I was greeted by large obtrusive signs, erected by our government employees, probably at great cost to the taxpayer, explaining that Aubrey Falls had been turned off. *Turned off? How could a waterfall be turned off?* On closer inspection, the falls had, in fact, disappeared entirely. There was a modest trickle oozing from a crevasse in the mighty shield of rock that once hosted a magnificent fall of water. I was staring at a blank, grey wall. Grey Owl would not have been pleased. As it turned out, the river had been dammed, *or should I say damned*, above the falls.

I inquired about the route from Bisco to Aubrey, believing that a trip down the Mississaga could be salvaged, at least away from road and rail, through Archie's wilderness. An associate friend had done it the year before and he was none too pleased with what he had encountered. Logging operations, which were underway at several points along the river, had eradicated many of the traditional portages, while clearcut operations close to the riverbank, at least visible from the water, had left hillsides bare except for the stumps and slash of trees. The sound of skidders and chainsaws reverberated through the river valley and hastily erected bridges were constructed at shallow rapids, not high enough to paddle under, yet jammed full of beaver cut and river floaters so that the bridge acted more like a dam than a bridge crossing for logging trucks.

Upon hearing all this I quickly lost my enthusiasm to explore Grey Owl's river, crossing it off my list of places to explore. And here, yet, is another cry of disdain for the loss of a once great river, kept alive now through the written word only, symbolic of man's greed and callous nature. And I have been to other rivers, dead to the world, save for a mere trace of the vitality they once heralded. One by one, rivers vanish, like endangered species, slipping off the face of existence.

Canada is rife with wild rivers; it was a great honour to have travelled down many of these soulful watery pathways by canoe; each river being noticeably different; each venture down a single river palpable by perspective and insight. And it takes several trips down a river to feel its moods and vagaries, to be consumed by the landscape that shapes and moulds its presence.

One venture, one quick-fire flash down the rapids for self-patronizing reasons, for the adrenalin rush, is not a communion with the soul of the river. You see nothing, and the river reveals nothing of itself. But to take the time, to hesitate and re-explore, perhaps to pole your canoe up the river for a change, is to experience another facet of the life of a river. Water is transparent. When you see the rapid and the flume of yellow-white water cresting, look more closely and you will see the rock that creates the dance of water over and around it; listen to the music, as strings to a violin, the rocks and ledges craft the movement of water into art, both visual and audible.

River walking is an acquired preference. In the city it would be explained as one about to step onto an escalator, but instead of being carried along at a given speed, you would be stepping backward, slowly, yet still being carried forward, but at a pace in which you could actually take in your surroundings.

I have mapped out many Canadian rivers, assessing the dangerous components, the rapids and falls, locations of portages and such, and have a partiality to exploring, in particular, the rugged and ragged nature of each obstruction in the river. I shouldn't say "obstruction," as there is nothing, save a concrete dam, that could hold back a river; the obstruction is merely an idiomatic label recording locations where one has to portage the canoe or assess whether a canoe can be navigated through without hardship. Walking the shoreline at such places, away from the trodden portage trail, is sometimes quite difficult, if not treacherous; yet it is through the labyrinth of rock and rubble, pitchholes, kettle depressions, fissures, gneissic lineaments, funnels, and carved-out channels that you find real beauty in dangerous places.

Many portage paths lead away from falls, chutes, and canyons, depriving the traveller of the opportunity to feel the very spirit of the river in its most grandiloquent mood. People are in a hurry, always, to get to the end of the trail and move on. Some do loiter and take the side trails that at least offer a glimpse of the river's passionate side, or camp by the canyon's edge or on the lip of the abyss overlooking a fall, taking in the full furor of the river. For some, sleep is elusive and fitful here, the voice of river spirits pervasive and headstrong with an enveloping aura of anxiousness that implores animals to take a wide birth around and birds to bypass.

In the far northwest, the Coppermine River wends its way to the Arctic Ocean, on occasion slipping noisily through canyons that rise two hundred feet above the maelstrom of rapids, ledges, and boils. Canoeists are required to portage far in advance of the canyons, climbing up to the tundra heath for some distance, several kilometres in some cases, before dropping back to the calmer pools below. Others have died trying to run the rapids.

Looking down from above, beside a stone marker and grim epitaph to the drowned canoeists, the river is menacing. But something compels you to go; to make the run, but not for bravado's sake or the fact that you don't have to carry all your equipment overland that would take half the day to accomplish; no, it's something unexplainable — the appeal of experiencing yet another face of the river; to feel the power and pull, the surge and swell of so much water compressed between the vault of rock and hurled downward at breakneck speed. It can be done.

The two canoes were tied together using stout spruce poles, catamaran-style, with a gap of two-feet between them and spray covers fastened over the open hulls. Pushing off, the canoes are swept away quickly — there is no turning back. We move steadily toward the gate entrance to the deep canyon, whitewater visible now, rising in pulsating fountains as the river plunges out of sight. There is no contest here, no conquering heroes, just a humble craft and four bright-eyed, fearful — not fearless — paddlers.

The canoe is manoeuvred to avoid a souse-hole that would engulf both canoes in a single breath with no chance of rescue; a quick sideslip to centre channel and a rollercoaster ride over two-metre swells for two kilometres. I'm leaning on the paddle, steering a course into the thick of it; I hook my thumb around the gunnel and lock the paddle tight to the side of the hull, and the canoes hold to the line of standing waves marking the right channel.

The noise is deafening; communication is futile but everyone knows what to do. It is at this moment when everything becomes stationary. I lean back on my paddle and look up at the cliffs, the serried cliff edge yellow-brown against a cerulean-blue sky; laying there I look straight up and I can see the tops of both sides of the river in peripheral perspective — a strange phenomenon saved only for canyons like this. A rock can be pitched across the span of the canyon.

Someone yells, *"ledge ahead!"* and we all pry and sweep and draw and the boats heel and come around in a tight upstream cross-ferry, and for a moment we are looking upstream back through the canyon from where we came and all you see are breaking white waves in angry profusion. The canoes are brought around and we slip past a deadly hydraulic where the two canoeists perished; water trapped within itself, rolling in against impervious rock, thrust out again only to be re-circulated back, again and again. The canyon turns, arcs right, sunlight on the cliffs in dappled streaks accentuating the pockmarks and fissures; rivulets spewing out from fractures shower the cliff face, leaving black streaks of lichen-crusted velvet that glisten like phosphorous. It's overwhelming and sensual; the undulating movements, the rhythm of paddles moving in unison, and a spectacular landscape witnessed by only a handful of people.

The perilous landscape of the canyon shifts to one of recumbent calm. Paddles ease into light strokes, breathing is more relaxed, and we have time to contemplate what just transpired. We had hiked and explored the brim of the gorge and the environs beyond, pondered carefully the run of the rapids below, and surreptitiously entered the abyss.

But the appeal and magnetism of such river landscapes and the element of risk sometimes impede the true meaning of river walking; getting caught up in the rush and disregarding the other nuances of wild landscapes. It would have been different had we not already explored the bluff edge, taking in the world from another perspective. Some rush headlong down the river under the guide of "quest" and not "journey." River walking is all about the journey.

13

MOUNTAINS

First two weeks on the job and already a climber fell to his death just off the Dart Track, and they just found some body parts of a Russian woman just below Dart hut who didn't make a stream crossing, even though she was repeatedly warned not to continue her tramp. A guide fell off a bluff near the Routeburn last season and I just heard a Warden in Fiordland National Park just died. Might be a busy season ...
— Michel Boulay, Department of Conservation,
New Zealand, Facebook, September 2009

"Ha, Archie, you've never been to the mountains, have you?" I asked.

"So what," Archie Grey Owl answered, taken aback by the question.

"Well, you give people the impression that you've been there and all." I loved catching Owl off-guard; he always wanted to be in control of the conversation.

"What are you getting at, shaganash?"

"Page 214 of Men of the Last Frontier — *the mountain picture, nice shot, where'd it come from?"*

"I don't remember. I think the publisher picked it out," Archie answered.

"And page 234, the Indian encampment at the foot of a mountain. And pages 13 and 20 and page 54 — your first book is full of mountain pictures, Archie." I was definitely getting under his skin. Archie was red in the face.

*"And in chapter one, 'The Vanguard,' you say that Canadian 'mountains have been conquered'... what do you mean by that, and how **does** one actually **conquer** a mountain?"*

"It's a manner of speaking, deliberately, shaganash, to make a point," Owl defended himself.

"And Riding Mountain National Park ... there are no mountains in Manitoba, Owl," I went on. *"You don't know anything about Canadian mountains, huh, Archie?"*

Archie had disappeared. Just like him whenever I had him up against the wall. *I'm one up on you Archie Grey Owl.* Not that it was an earth-shaking revelation or acclaim to any glory. Owl pushed me to press the limits since I was a kid, and it was my way to let him know that I did exactly what he impressed upon me to do.

I sat at one of the tables in the outfitter's café drinking a beer, waiting for a floatplane ride up to my cabin. The teenager behind the desk was trying to make himself understood to an attractive, tall brunette as to what canoe route she and her boyfriend should take. He really didn't have a clue and she picked up on his indifference.

"Talk to the guy drinking the beer, he'll know." The teenager pointed at me. The woman ordered a beer, grabbed the route map, and sat down at my table.

"Hi, I'm Sonya. Apparently you can help me," she said matter-of-factly.

Sonya and her boyfriend, Michel, had been in Canada for a few weeks and wanted to top off their visit with a month-long canoe trip before heading back to New Zealand. Michel, a transplanted Québécois, had been working as a park warden and trail-builder for the Department of Conservation for over a decade, manning a trail hut on one of the popular hiking trails; Sonya was German but had grown up in Thailand, and was working as a trail guide in New Zealand.

I marked out a route for a month-long paddle, offering the use of my cabin as a rest stop-over. They accepted the proposal, left, and I never saw them again until my plane landed in Queenstown, New Zealand, the following May. I had paddled in to my cabin that summer to find a note from the two of them, thanking me for letting them use the place. There was also an invitation to come to New Zealand as a guest park warden — an offer I found difficult to refuse.

At the time, I was looking for solitude; to get away as far as I could possibly go. To be in a new, strange land appealed to my sense of self-preservation and sanity. I also wanted to be in the mountains. I had, up to then, experienced shades of mountain serenity, to feel and think the landscape in finite terms and distant pleasures. Mountains were always only in the background, or fleeting glimpses from an aircraft or vehicle. The offer to go to New Zealand presented the panacea to woo the spirit and challenge the soul. It would be a minimalist venture; I had little money left from an expensive divorce, and I wanted dearly to forget the misery that woman put me through — to forget women altogether.

Alone. Just me and the mountains, on the other side of the world.

I was bone tired after the long flight from Los Angeles. My cold had now moved into my lungs and all I wanted to do was sleep. The jet landed in Auckland on the North Island, still a thousand miles from my destination. A buzzer went off as my carry-on bag was put through the scanner in customs.

"Sir, what's this in your carry-on?" An officious female voice was barely registering. They put my bag through the scanner again.

"I don't know … a pair of socks?" I answered.

That was the wrong answer. The woman waved for a uniformed officer to escort me off to a side table. I was told to empty my bag. A green apple and a carrot fell on to the table — my lunch that I was supposed to eat before landing.

"Do you understand you signed a declaration saying that you were not bringing any fruit into New Zealand, sir?" the officer said. I made up some excuses but nothing seemed to be working, short of a bribe. In New Zealand, where few things are indigenous, they take this stuff seriously. It cost me two hundred dollars — half of the only money I had left to keep me for a month. *Welcome to New Zealand!*

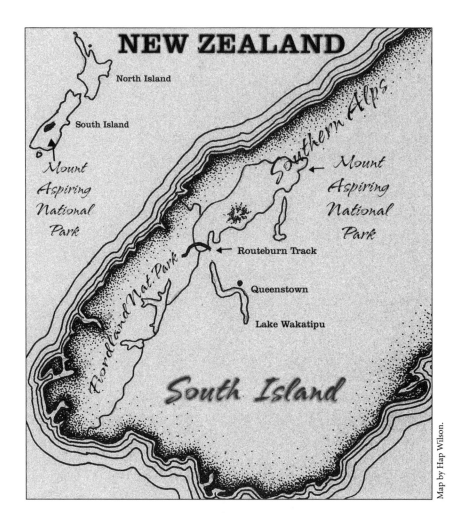

SOUTH ISLAND, NEW ZEALAND.

Michel and Sonya were at the airport when I landed in Queenstown. Like half the population of New Zealand, they drove a used van. Every other vehicle was a VW microbus or slowly degrading four-by-four or minivan. I purchased my supplies and we headed north to Glenorchy, where Michel was building a house. It was also the home office for the Department of Conservation.

New Zealand is famous for its mountain treks, and the government spent millions building elaborate trails, huts, and suspension bridges through the Southern Alps. The warden service and the huts were generally shut down by the end of April, but the popular Routeburn Track saw enough fringe season use to keep the hut open through the month of May. They felt comfortable with me since I had winter survival certification; I would be their first "test" guest warden. My job was simple: take trampers' hut tickets, make sure the hut fire is going at night, and radio in to head office each morning. The rest of the day would be mine.

Luckily, a DOC helicopter was heading up to the Falls hut with a trail-building crew, and they had offered to take one of my food packs. I said I'd carry my other pack, since it had most of my personal gear in it; that turned out to be a mistake. It was still seventy-five pounds and my cold had stripped me of the energy to make the ten-kilometre hike in on the Routeburn. I had brought along a spare tent and climbing equipment — crampons and ice axe, borrowed from my friend Peggy Foster who had approached the Everest summit on more than one occasion. She was kind enough to share some advice and the extra equipment. I had scant knowledge of the tracks but I did know that the weather could be much like that of a northern Ontario November.

I was in the deep valley of Nan Curunir — "the Wizard's vale" — at the roots of Methedras, the last peak of the Misty Mountains, and the River Isen flowed through the vale in shallow braids. North of Glenorchy, above Lake Wakatipu, we crossed near the junction of the Routeburn and Rees River, tributaries of the famous Dart River. This was the movie-scene location for Isengard in the trilogy *Lord of the Rings*. But Mount Earnslaw was in the background, not Methedras, and it would be this mountain I would wake up to greet each morning from my warden's hut.

The staff at the DOC office in Glenorchy was enthusiastic about having their first "guest" warden occupy the hut on the Routeburn. I was even outfitted with a crested park shirt, shorts, and fleece. *National Geographic Adventure* magazine had just voted the Routeburn Track as one of the world's top eleven trails, and of all the mountain trails, the Routeburn was the busiest in the shoulder season, even busier now with all the hoopla and notoriety. But according to Michel, who was now leading the way ahead of me up this mountain trail with a pace that would rival a long-distance runner, the Routeburn also attracted the neophyte hiker. People died along the track at regular periods; and the risk was higher in May because of the potential for hypothermia and dangerous ice conditions through the mountain passes.

I had limited climbing experience. I did some "free-climbing" years ago; climbing semi-technical ascents without equipment, even in bare feet in order to get a better purchase on the rocks. Crazy stuff. I stopped after one near-death experience on a climb in Alberta. I wasn't afraid of heights, but my lack of technical climbing experience would be enough to limit what I would or could do in New Zealand. But with the state of mind I was currently in — post-marital depression and financial stress — I was prone to ignoring the usual sensibilities as they applied to proper personal safety protocol. The thought of my two children back home in Canada was the only leavening agent in my psyche at the time, and the thought of them being brought up by my ex-wife and her narcissistic parents (if I were to succumb to my actions), was unimaginable.

Out of shear stubbornness I kept up to Michel's racing pace, although I thought I was going to die somewhere along the steep trail. I now had a fever and had to stop every few hundred metres to catch my breath, then jog for ten minutes to catch up to Michel. He was in top shape after a Kiwi summer doing trail work, whereas I had just spent a some- what lethargic winter doing studio illustrations; capped-off with a severe lung-infection, I was in no condition to do much of anything except to lie down and sleep.

After the second suspension bridge, both obvious and necessary structures, we stopped at what looked like an arroyo. It was also a good chance to get him to stop and let me rest.

"There's not a lot of rain on this side of the mountains, but when it does rain," Michel explained, "these rivers and creeks become dangerous torrents. Trampers get killed trying to cross these streams." Good point to remember; many of the creeks were not bridged along some of the tracks and you were often required to make crossings with good judg- ment, or even turn back if the rivers were flooded.

We were following an historic track called the "bridle path" built in the 1870s, first to supply an old blacksmith camp, and a decade later to cater to an influx of tourists. Before Europeans discovered the Routeburn

Valley, people of the Tai Poutini iwi travelled up the river gorge to access pounamu jade, used for tool making, weaponry, and ornaments. Tourists used horses to travel up the trail as far as the "flats" — a large, grassy plateau valley at the foot of the Humboldt Mountain range. From here, a rough trail was carved out to allow guided hikes up to Harris Saddle — a beautiful mountain pass and highest point along the track.

But it is the side trips where people get themselves into trouble — up the Valley of Trolls, or attempting to shortcut across to the McKenzie Hut, climbing Conical Hill and slipping off a precipice, or simply pushing their energy and time limits and getting caught between huts, exhausted and cold. According to Michel, international trampers seriously underestimate the vagaries of the mountain weather; the trail starts in a veritable rainforest-like, lush environment, and as you climb higher, beyond the treeline, you are confronted with a subarctic climate.

From the flats to the Routeburn Falls hut is a 2.5-kilometre, steady, steep climb, up past Eagle Cliff (where a group of Israeli hikers got stranded for a couple of days), over a suspension bridge spanning Emily Creek, and across a major slip (rockfall) that took out part of the trail in 1987.

"You have to make your way up the creek, a thousand vertical feet to Emily Pass, and it's a shortcut to the Mackenzie Hut." Michel pointed out all the features along the way. Every time he talked, we had a chance to rest; my lungs were burning and I was about to pass out. "Not far," Michel would say at each new bend in the trail. The Routeburn Valley slipped away below us, casually visible through breaks in the forest canopy, framed in by the Humboldt Mountains, Mount Momus, and Mount Somnus, snow-packed and glistening in the late afternoon sun. The air was cooler now, and the sweat that ran down my back was more from the fever than the toil of the carry. The hut, finally, came into view — a veritable five-star hostel perched near the rock pitch-off to the valley, several hundred feet below. I could hear Routeburn Falls tumbling into its grotto above the cabins, coursing pell-mell over the precipice to the valley. I had arrived in paradise.

The warden's cabin was separate from the forty-bunk hut; replete with on-demand hot water, solar-powered lights and radio system, and propane stove; the cabin slept five rangers. The trampers' hut was still open for visitors, but the water and propane had been shut off. Michel had warned me to watch that my own water lines didn't freeze up soon, but I could enjoy a hot shower for another couple of weeks anyway.

"You can trade off hot showers for necessities," Michel announced. Apparently, some trampers come well-provisioned, and a hot shower is worth a lot to grubby hikers.

"You'd be amazed at what you can barter for," Michel said as he pointed out a box of condoms on the bookshelf. The pantry was still well-stocked and I was to help myself to what was there. That was a good thing, as I brought only basic food for the month, and as it turned out, I could put in an order to DOC in Glenorchy for a re-provision in a couple of weeks and they'd fly it up to the hut for me. This was too good to be true.

Beneath the lower pantry shelf were at least a dozen two-litre Pepsi bottles of homemade stout that Michel had brewed during the summer.

"You can either drink it or toss it," Michel said. "It might be a bit skunky."

Michel left the next morning. I slept most of the day, trying to shake off the chest cold; the mountain air seemed to work like an elixir, and the realization that I was alone in a mountain cabin in one of the most beautiful places in the world still hadn't sunk in.

"Kay-yaa, kay-yaa!"

I woke up to this awful screeching noise outside the cabin. Of anything wild in New Zealand, the only creature to be watchful of was the thing railing outside my door. Unlike Australia, where there are more creatures that will kill you than any other country in the world, New Zealand has none.

"Watch out for the kea," Michel had warned. They'll sometimes land on the backs of snow-bound sheep and eat away at their kidneys while they're still alive."

Good information to be forewarned about. The kea is the only alpine parrot in the world and its call is unmistakeable. Several large, stocky, olive-green parrots wearing red underwear had descended on the cabin, pecking away at something on the roof. Keas were basically vegetarian, using their powerful beaks to pry open tough seeds and to root into the ground; they ate berries and the nectar of mountain flax and rata flowers ... and the kidneys of stranded sheep on occasion. Most of all, they were a nuisance.

"Don't leave your hiking boots outside, or anything else for that matter," Michel had warned. Kea are inquisitive birds and have been known to pull apart window caulking on vehicles, rip apart tents, chew the stitching out of boots, steal food, and, as they were doing right now, pulling out the rubber gasket material from the solar panels on the roof.

Running outside to chase them off, it was the first time I had a sense of where I was. I quickly forgot about the kea.[7]

The morning sun had worked its way down the west side of the Humboldt Range in bright orange alpen-glow; Mount Earnslaw (2,819 metres), New Zealand's second-highest mountain, pierced the east horizon with its double peaks as a mist rose up from the valley floor in long, ghost-like ribbons.

Archie, you really missed out on this, I thought. It felt good to be out of Canada, to be doing something so different, so far away, in a wilderness where you felt so insignificant in the scope of things. No phones, no emails, no threatening letters from the Canada Revenue Agency. And the mountains were approachable here, close and intimate and luring, the valleys beckoning to be discovered, mountain streams that ran emerald clear and cold, and birds that wore red underwear. My soul was stripped naked. Just me and the mountains and ...

"Hey, get some clothes on!" someone shouted from the hut balcony. A group of trampers were enjoying their morning coffee on the deck, at least until I came crashing out of the warden's hut, stark naked and waving my arms at the kea. Laughter.

I put on my official warden-wear and collected their overnight passes. Ten bucks for the off-season; a good deal when it was forty during the tramping season, and you had to book in advance. I had to get used to people dropping in to the hut. I wasn't alone.

---

7   In Archie's world, the antics of the kea could easily be compared with the mischievous mannerisms of the Whiskey Jack, also known as the Canada Jay, Grease Bird, and Camp Robber.

After the morning radio chat with the Glenorchy base, I had the rest of the day to myself. I would pack a lunch, a mountain chart showing the tracks and passes and elevation data, a first-aid kit and PLB (personal locator beacon). I was to use the PLB in case of an emergency, either for myself or an injured tramper.

I needed to familiarize myself with the track, at least the section between the flats hut, through the falls hut and beyond, up through the Harris Saddle, and down into the basin where the Lake Mackenzie hut was located, a distance of about twenty kilometres. The track was thirty-eight kilometres in length, linking the Hollyford and Routeburn valleys via the Harris Saddle; it was touted as New Zealand's most popular trans-alpine track. Even though the trail was well-marked and graded, it was impassable at times due to more than thirty avalanche zones, heavy snows, and ice conditions. May was the start of the Kiwi winter, and conditions could vary from warm tropic-like weather in the valleys to numbing snow squalls through the upper pass.

It was a different world above the falls hut. The lush beech forests terminated here; somewhat of a physiographic anomaly, the actual treeline is an abrupt demarcation at the one-thousand-metre elevation, giving the mountains an obvious and conspicuous two-tone appearance. Dark verdant forest gives way to tawny snow tussock and shrublands. The treeline is an edgy place due to the severity of the climate — beech forests cannot invade the alpine shrublands or grassy plateaus, and, conversely, the alpine ecology is thwarted by the thick shade of the forests. Snow or rock avalanches cut swathes through the treeline at regular intervals.

Oddly enough, there are more plant species within the alpine zone than in the lower, warmer valleys. In an environment that would be considered inhospitable, where snow can fall at any time during the year, the flora is diverse and tenacious. At the onset of winter, the herbs and cushion plants have a distinct russet visage; but at close observation there is an explosion of sub-colours and earth tones that define a multifarious ecology, fragile and delicate by nature but extremely resolute.

The steep rise to the Harris Saddle, in part, was blasted out of the side of the cliff; ice conditions made this stretch treacherous. The wind was sharp here, diminishing the effects of the sun. The emergency hut at the apex of the Saddle was a smart move by the DOC in minimizing the potential for hypothermic incidents; yet people still succumbed here, often enough by getting off the track or misreading conditions.

I climbed Conical Hill from the Saddle — a steep monolithic outcrop that rose several hundred feet above the pass and gave a 360-degree view of the track, of the Routeburn Valley, and an impressive view of the Hollyford Valley, through to Lake McKerrow, Martin's Bay, and the Tasman Sea. This was Sir Edmund Hillary's backyard — the Darran Range — Mount Madeline and Mount Tutoko, impressive peaks where Hillary practiced before climbing Mount Everest. A cold wind assaulted the isolated zenith of the rock hill and it wasn't long before a bone-deep chill set in and I had to get moving again. Walking back slowly through the grassland plateau, I watched as the late afternoon sun scaled the west-facing ridges. Darkness came quickly to the Routeburn. I would climb Conical on several occasions during my stay, once clambering up on my hands and knees, probing for hand-holds up a sheer iced-over trail.

There was scant firewood at the hut, except what could be collected through the nearby beech forest. Wardens used coal, primarily, to heat the cabins. I would ration the wood I had to start fires only, or to get a fire going in the trampers' hut if anyone showed up. Nights were cold and I had shut the water supply off after the first week because I was afraid the lines would freeze; so much for bartering hot showers with trampers.

As it turned out, most hikers opted to sleep next to the stove in the main room, rather than in the unheated bunk rooms. My cabin was small and maintained a comfortable temperature, and I shared the warmth with many of the trampers who were ill-prepared, loaned them extra fleece jackets and gloves for their trek, which they kindly returned on their hike back. The main dining room in the trampers' hut was inordinately large for the stove to have any effect. Each late afternoon I would fire up the stove, enough to radiate a friendly glow in the perimeter area, and when the trampers arrived they would camp beside the stove, and I would join them in the evening with a bottle of Michel's skunky stout, and we would share stories, songs, and revelations about the beauty of the New Zealand mountains.

It would often snow, and I would wake up to yet another world, a world that altered the sepia landscape to one of white wonder. The deeper snow in the alpine valley above the hut obfuscated the life forms that defined New Zealand as a land apart — the remnant Mount Cook Lily, the kotukutuku and pineapple shrubs, the hardy edelweiss; now it resembled an Arctic or Antarctic landscape, devoid of all life forms; even the greyschist — exposed rock blown clear of snow by intense wind — sparkles with the ice-like glistening of embedded mica flakes. Up close, along the trail to the pass, the rushes, cushion plants, and sedges are thick with ice, showy in their temporal wraps.

The trail is treacherous. Thick ice coats the rock and it takes steady footing to remain upright. There are few handholds to rely on. The sun is just rising, and I walk back to the hut to write the weather report and trail conditions on the info board. Trampers are just getting up; they moan when they see the snow. By the time they reach the Harris Saddle, the snow will be gone. The ice on the trail will remain longer.

DANGER,
ICE CONDITIONS PREVAIL THROUGH THE
PASS AND UP CONICAL HILL

Trampers gathered around the sign board. I'd make a visual checklist of their clothing and make comments when I saw hikers wearing blue jeans, sneakers, or inadequate outer clothing. Few trampers were well-prepared; most were visiting students on temporary work visas from the United States, Germany, Israel, and Canada, adding the hike up the Routeburn to their "to-do" list, grabbing what essentials they needed for a casual trek, not really thinking about, or researching fully, the type of conditions they may encounter in the mountains. The Kiwis, on the other hand, mostly up from the Queenstown area, were well-versed in mountain-wear protocol; an older assemblage of adventure seekers, they were always fun to be with, and it always exacted an extra bottle of beer and tunes on the harmonica in the dining hall.

I was exhausted after each day. I would walk at least twenty kilometres, always to a new and different destination — up a valley or to climb a rise or follow a creek. I would get back to the hut at dusk, collect tickets, chat with trampers, and, if it looked like a responsive group, sit and share stories, drink beer, bum chocolate or coffee, sing, and play the harmonica.

Word soon got out in Queenstown to the head office of the Department of Conservation that the Canadian warden at Routeburn was a real party fellow that put on quite a show. That would normally have sparked curiosity and a visit by a supervisor, but most of what was related dealt with how well the trampers were treated; the already warming fires lit in the stove, the offer of extra clothing, the shelter of my own cabin for those in dire need. By the end of each day I was exhausted, happy, and I would retreat to my cabin, write in my journal, and, with a Cheshire cat grin, fall asleep. In the morning I would be awakened by the screeching cacophony of demented mountain parrots.

"You have it made here, shaganash," Archie said.

"What are you doing here? I thought you didn't like the mountains, Owl. This is my gig, anyway," I said, somewhat on edge. Except for the voice, Archie had transmogrified into a techy trekker, sporting a North Face jacket, Gore-Tex bibs, and fleece cap, braids held back in a double ponytail.

"You should get a full-time job here, work for the government ... get a regular paycheque." Archie helped himself to a slug from my only bottle of scotch.

"Easy on that — it has to last me a month, Archie." I took a swig and pushed the bottle under my bunk.

"If it weren't for my kids back home, I'd do it. The DOC guys aren't like the bureaucrat goons back home."

"Tell me about it," Archie said.

"You had it good, too, Archie, at Ajawaan, in Prince Albert National Park." Archie went sombre. Silence. I handed Archie the scotch.

"There were moments," Archie lamented, *"when I wanted to kill myself."*

"What did you expect, Archie? The super gave you a lot of leeway — you were a government employee who spent half his time on benders in Prince Albert," I said.

"*What would you have done, shaganash, in my boots? You're no different than me. I pimped myself out for the Parks. I was their whore, selling myself and the beavers to the world just to sell park passes … make the government boys look good,*" Archie said with an air of defiance.

"*At least you didn't have to wear a uniform,*" I said.

"*They bought me hook, line, and sinker — the whole package. I was a better sell dressed in buckskins than pressed park duds. Anyway, I didn't look Indian at all when I wore white man's clothes. You, shaganash, you didn't get along with your supervisors either.*"

"*I admit I could get testy,*" I confessed, "*especially under a heavy deadline.*"

"*It was more than just deadlines, speeches, and books for me.*" Archie was almost yelling now, reaching again for the scotch.

"*You were moody, arrogant, imperious … not the gentle and sensitive woodsman in your books. The wardens hated you, at Crean and Kingsmere, they called you 'Bastard Grey Owl' or 'Hoot Owl.' You were doing good things, Archie, but you screwed up at the end.*"

"*Yes, I screwed up. Succinctly put, shaganash. And you know in your own life by what I mean to tell you.*" Archie took off his cap and let his ponytails down, rubbed his eyes with the end of his fingers. *Were his eyes watering?*

"*Pony, when she left, it destroyed a part of me,*" Archie said. "*She never liked it at Ajawaan … at least not enough to stay with me. She had this wanderlust. The adventure for us ended at Prince Albert, when I became famous. She didn't like being in my shadow.*" Archie picked at the frayed edges of skin on his fingers.

"*Archie, so, in Prince Albert where you carried on, got pissed — you were just another Indian to them. Nobody knew you there, so you got lost in the crowd, became a part of the thing you detested, really. Just another drunk Indian.*"

"*It's more complicated,*" Archie said. "*Pony became distant; and when she got pregnant with Dawn, she withdrew from me entirely. We lived together, separate lives at Ajawaan. Put on an act for the people. But it was mostly me they came to see — not Anahareo. She was often ignored, snubbed sometimes, pushed aside. I was too blind with my own ego to see what was happening.*"

"*And you flirted with the young women,*" I said.

"*Yes.*"

"*And you would argue, later, with Pony.*"

"*Terrible arguments.*"

"*Why would she want to stay, Archie? You drove her away. In the end she saw a broken down man who was nothing like the one she learned to love — the man she would snowshoe through the dead of night, forty miles, to live in a mouse-ridden trapper's cabin in the middle of the wilderness with.*" I could feel Archie's pain. I had suffered through the same love pitfalls, where ego and frustration manipulated everything I did, and I began to hide behind the truth. And it all gets worse, and you wonder why the love fades and regret pollutes your every thought.

"*The writing, the lectures ... it was all that was left of the man. I became the story, had to because I could no longer do the things I once could — lift the canoe, carry the load, my feet would swell up, my knees were shot. I was in pain most of the time. It made me edgy and morose, frustrated, angry with myself.*" I could tell Archie wasn't finished.

"*The ruse ... it was just about up. I knew it was coming to an end, soon. I didn't know how to deal with it if I were alive.*"

"*What do you mean, Archie? You killed yourself?*" I questioned.

"*More or less. I didn't really care anymore, about myself, my health. That's why I drank so much. I was so tired; the lectures were hard for me. I was always expecting someone to yell from the audience that I was a charlatan. I had dreams, no, nightmares about it.*"

"*And then Anahareo left you,*" I said.

"*Yes, both of us, Dawn and me. She said she needed to find herself,*" Archie said.

"*Archie, young women do this. You should have seen this coming, maybe prepared yourself instead of getting angry and depressed. Archie, Anahareo was a budding feminist way ahead of her time ... you both were visionaries. She needed her independence and you had to get the message out about the state of the wilderness.*"

"*You've got a good thing going here, shaganash.*" Archie stood up, put his cap on and left. It was snowing.

The next day a young Québécois lad showed up. He had come from the Mackenzie hut, over Emily Pass, staggering into the dining hall. He said he was going to make the twelve-kilometre trek back to Mackenzie where his gear was left. It was nearly dark and his clothes and shoes were soaking wet. I made him stay in the warden's cabin with me; he realized he wouldn't have made it otherwise.

He returned a few days later and we made some excursions together, long ones, tough hikes, one thirty-eight kilometres long that took us over Sugar Loaf Mountain and down into the Rock Burn River, over to the Dart Valley, around beautiful Lake Sylvan, and as far as the flats hut. We didn't have the energy left for the steep climb up to the falls hut. I told my trail mate that the flats hut was well-provisioned, with food and sleeping bags and even a couple cello-paks of wine. When we got there, cold and hungry, we discovered to our apprehension that the DOC staff had removed all the provisions for the winter, except for two wool blankets and a part container of dry soup powder. The temperature had plunged well below freezing and it was a chore to keep the cabin heated throughout the long night.

It was easy to understand how trampers perished out here, overestimating their abilities on trails that demanded the utmost care; crossing streams, ice and snow pack, precipitous climbs, all eating up precious daylight hours. The shelters were far apart and it was necessary to execute a well-laid plan. It was a learning experience for me in a landscape that pressed all the buttons.

In all, I had trekked over 350 kilometres through Aspiring National Park and into Fiordland. I had climbed up to Emily Pass after a heavy snow, dodging rockfall that would have easily crushed my skull if I misjudged my steps, and with the ice axe and crampons managed to reach the apex just to enjoy the view into the Mackenzie Valley. The thought of dying off-trail, like so many others had, crossed my mind enough to make me aware of the risks.

Through the valley of trolls, around Lake Harris, I made my way up to the headwaters of the Routeburn, to Wilson Lake, spending the day basked in mountain sunlight, on top of the world. The lake was black, as if looking into a great bottomless hole, unfrozen, contrasted by steep-sided, snow-packed ridges and a sky, blue to the point of being surreal. The overwhelming feeling of aloneness, and the realization that I could never fully relate the sensation of being at this place, photographically, or by the written word, could be conveyed true to its dimension, was, in fact, a great epiphany for me. As a writer and a photographer it could be a paradoxical dilemma; or perhaps I wasn't good enough at either to adequately capture the experience; but I didn't care. I stopped taking pictures and put my journal away and sat against a large boulder in the sun. Soon enough I melted away into the landscape of the mountains.

There is something of the sublime in feeling trivial in the realm of great landscapes. It is truly the only place you can actually sense your consignment in the greater portrait of life. The world takes on an old perspective, contrary to the modern world, made small by technology; and instead of feeling "crowded" and unimportant, the vastness of the Earth around gives rise to an almost overwhelming preponderance of self-gratification and thankfulness.

14

BOREALIS

Here and there, too, the sable carpet of evergreen tree-tops is gashed by long shining ribbons of white, as mighty rivers tumble and roar their way to Hudson's Bay, walled in on either side by their palisades of spruce trees, whose lofty arches give back the clatter of rapids or echo to the thunder of the falls …
— Grey Owl, *Men of the Last Frontier*, "Land of Shadows"

Boreas was the purple-winged god of the north wind — one of the four directional *Anemoi* (wind-gods) in Greek mythology. Boreas was also god of winter, who would sweep down from the cold mountains of Thrake, chilling the air with his icy breath. In post-classical art, particularly found adorning the top corner of old maps, Boreas appears from the clouds, puffed cheeks blowing a gust of wind. In Canada, Boreas claims ownership to three-quarters of the total forested lands, or one-third of this essential resource globally.

Wrapped around like a thousand-kilometre-wide green scarf, the boreal forest drapes the country, from the Yukon to Labrador, and is Canada's largest biome (environmental community). It extends across Scandinavia and Russia as the Taiga — known as the land between the subarctic to the north and the deciduous forest to the south. Because of the climate conditions, the boreal forest is found only in the northern hemisphere. From a global perspective, this biome comprises 25 percent of the world's closed canopy forest; because of its immensity, the amount of carbon dioxide absorbed and stored, and the oxygen released, the boreal forest is a huge player in the mitigation of global warming.

For as long as wasps have been on this Earth they have been making paper nests from their own spit and one other essential ingredient — a pulp made from chewed bits of wood fibre. It wasn't until the mid 1800s that humans figured out how to make paper from wood pulp; and the pulp most sought-after comes from the boreal forest. Each tree from the boreal forest, on average, yields about thirty-eight kilograms of fine paper, or seventy-five kilograms of newsprint. Each Canadian consumes several trees worth of paper products each year; every issue of the *Toronto Star*, for example, requires three hundred metric tonnes of newsprint ... bad news for the environment.

There's no question that the Canadian boreal forest is at risk, not just for its wood fibre, but for its resultant displacement of prime animal species such as the woodland caribou. Arbitrary park boundaries, sketched on a map to conform to forest company needs, define Woodland Caribou Park in Ontario, and its sister park in Manitoba, Atikaki. The park system is a gross contradiction in ideology and nomenclature, really having nothing whatsoever to do with protecting the endangered woodland caribou that reside inside and outside the parks. Like most wilderness and environment parks in Ontario, logging interests have shaved the forest clean up to the boundaries, with total disregard for caribou habitat.

But this isn't another enviro bash-the-corporate-evildoer essay; I'd rather talk about the landscape and other nuances that personify the boreal tracts of Canada. And there is delineation between boreal forest types, as well, not clearly marked as a line on a map, but separated in two categories depending on latitude and climate. At the Height of Land, where rivers flow north into Hudson Bay, just beyond the mixed deciduous forest, lies a seemingly endless flow of spruce in undulating rolls and sloughs, broken occasionally by rock outcrops. After all, this is still a sampling of the great Shield dome as it slides into the ocean. Rivers like the Missinaibi, the Abitibi, Harricanaw, Albany, Winisk, northward to the Hayes and Nelson, wend their way through the great spruce forests;

trees are packed tight together with little skyline definition except for a modest fine saw-cut edge. This is known as the Closed Crown Forest.

Approaching the treeline, which in itself can reach a varied width of several hundred kilometres, is the Land of Little Sticks. Here the trees form scabrous pockets of stunted black spruce, or generally scattered through-out as if the Earth was suffering from a case of scabies. In some places it is as desolate looking and foreboding as the tundra, and in others, surprisingly lush and welcoming. This is the subarctic, open lichen boreal forest.

It is a fire-dependent ecosystem; the forest requires fire to open the seed cones. Only a very small percentage of the seeds are cracked open by the heat of the sun alone. As one travels northwest, past Lake Superior, fire is more of a common occurrence within the boreal ranks. Having canoed through a great part of this region, it is exemplified as a patch-work of old and new fires; scorched sticks bleached white against white rock moraines, young Jack pine sprouting up from the rubble, growing so tight together as to make passage impossible. Mapping out a route through the Atikaki Reserve, I came upon a ten-year-old burn between the Sassaginigak and Leyond rivers; a devastating fire that left nothing of the mature trees or any indication of the location of traditional Native portages. Even the rocks still bore the scorch marks, and boulders that had exploded from the heat lay in broken piles, obstructing any advance-ment beyond. The two-metre-high Jack pine that had grown since the fire had pinioned themselves so tightly to the rocks, and in so dense a thicket, like bars in a jail cell, there was no way through but to spend the day with axe and saw to cut another portage. And after the labour of clearing a new trail, you would be black from head to toe with the soot from handling and walking through burnt timber. Sometimes you would paddle for half a day before clearing one fire swath, only to paddle an hour before hitting the next burn-over.

The boreal forest is a dynamic system of living organisms; plants, animals, insects, and micro-organisms, interacting with each other and the physical environment of soil, water, and air. Black spruce is the pre-dominant species; its short, waxy needles with branches tight to the trunk enable it to withstand the toughest of elements. White spruce also grow in preferred locations, and in north-central Manitoba I have seen these grow to a diameter of one metre or more and to a height of more than a hundred feet. Jack pine can be found wherever fire has passed though, mostly found on higher ground, while tamarack prefer the fenland border areas. There are some hardwoods here; a scattering of birch and poplar, diamond willow, alder, and mountain ash, which offer a splash of colour in the fall and the sound of rustling leaves in the summer wind.

I will say this of the boreal forest: I have had some of the best fishing along her rivers, in places where no motorized clubbers venture; fabulous whitewater, unobstructed for miles; but I've also had some of the worst campsites, toughest portages, the worst storms, and the most malevolent biting flies while canoeing its river corridors. It's a region of environmental extremes, indicative of the tenacity of its life forms.

Landscapes here are as variable as the weather. From the rock and Jack pine riverscapes typical of Manitoba's eastern rivers, like the Bloodvein, Gammon, Manigotagan, Berens, and Pigeon rivers — even the Hayes and Nelson rivers — you can suddenly find yourself wallowing in an endless morass of monotonous black spruce. From the air you get a much different perspective of the land and water mass than from the river itself; a bird's eye view reveals the montage of lowland fen, open rock terraces, and landlocked boreal ponds. Paddling these rivers proffer a more "structured" shoreline, rimmed by the familiar granite and gneissic rock outcrops, topped with scattered Jack pine. Bald eagles are prevalent here (seemingly to be found at every river bend) and so too are vultures; the fishing is good — for walleye, bass, pike, and channel catfish. Toward Lake Winnipeg, pelicans soar like kites high above the boreal tracts.

For the last 150 kilometres as these rivers approach Hudson Bay through Quebec, Ontario, and Manitoba, they become sluggish and wide, the landscape dreary, the water murky; most visitors would find it boring compared with the vivaciousness of the headwater areas. High, eroding clay banks obscure the forest, but from your vantage point the spruce are too thick anyway to see more than a couple of metres past the perimeter trees. Collapsed slopes signify the unstable nature of the river shore. Beyond the rim of the river, the slough of muskeg is like a sponge; the over-saturated weak points give way and slide into the river, carrying with them the forest matt and whatever trees attached to it.

The boreal forest that Archie became familiar with during his trapping days in northern Quebec was the more southerly crown forest, where remnant Shield rock was still prolific. The headwater region of the Abitibi and Matagami rivers, near the villages of Val d'Or, Malartic, Senneterre, and the Cree Reserve at Lac Simon, where Archie testified on behalf of two Native trappers, must have seemed like the end of the world … at least the end of the rail line north. It was two hundred kilometres northeast of his home territory of Temagami; an area already denuded of beaver. Beyond the familiar pine forests of Temagami and Biscotasing, known well to Archie, the Lac Simon region sported a more guaranteed harvest of beaver, and beaver thrived in this ecosystem better than in the pine lands. Here there were large tributary streams, feeder-creeks, and beaver ponds, interconnected by vast stretches of boreal grasslands and wet bogs. Wetland shores were lined with trembling aspen and birch — the foodstuff of the beaver.

Outside of winter it is treacherous territory to travel on by foot, if not impossible; movement by snowshoe, however, would be easy over packed snow trails. The uneven, log-choked ground is now buried under a metre of winter white; perilous conditions remained through the coldest winters as the ice thickness was seldom regular and beaver environments presented the most inauspicious footing. When Archie coerced and charmed Anahareo to his winter cabin here, she would have found the landscape depressing, adding to the already heavy conflicts they shared in the small shack. It wouldn't have been the sort of place any apprentice would simply don snowshoes and trek off into the wilds. Travel would have been restricted to tight creek corridors and shallow beaver ponds where winter ice was often thin and unreliable, especially near beaver dam outlets. Anahareo discovered this the hard way by nearly succumbing after falling through lake ice.

Anahareo may have been a debutant outdoorswoman, naive to the ways of the trail, but Archie was almost adolescent in his scope of understanding women who fall quickly in love with an ideal. To think love alone, infatuation with the façade of romance in the wilds, could bond into a healthy relationship was ludicrous on both their parts. Gertrude was young, but ripe to find a swashbuckling hero of fairytale romances;

Archie was lustful and easily enamoured by pretty girls. No doubt, as Archie approached middle-age, he was insecure about a lot of things; he, better than most, as an educated man, should have known that the hardship of trail and trapping life would curtail any sense of romantic bliss. Winters were long, and the trapping trade brutal, as Anahareo soon found out, and her imaginary hero quickly turned into the heartless killer.

Stepping aside from the winter harshness of boreal land and climate, the best way to enjoy the crown forest is by summer canoe trip. Notwithstanding the intensity of the blackflies, mosquitoes, deer and horseflies, all of which thrive in this moist ecosystem, you can find respite within the open waters or windy points by day and the cooler hours of the late evening. Shield boreal campsites are often perched on ledge rock with a fine view of the rapids below and with just enough of a breeze to scatter pesky flies. Firewood is plentiful, borrowed from the tops of old beaver lodges or cut from past fire sites on your way through, as it is against the code of the trail to denude the vicinity of the campsite of ready fuel. In the evening it is hard to see the canopy of stars because of the closeness of the forest unless you find a camp on the lower boreal stretches atop a sand bar or gravel bank, but you do get the odd glimpse of the "Dance of the Deadmen" Archie wrote about — the Aurora Borealis or Northern Lights with their ghostlike tendrils, phosphorescent, almost audibly hissing, dancing their macabre dance across the sky. There is no better place on Earth to experience this than floating in a canoe, bound to a boreal river.

The toil of the portage is made easier by the beauty of the cathedral-like palisade of stately trees, festooned with Old Man's Beard lichen. The old forest here and the climate provide the perfect environment for both lichen and sphagnum moss, the latter of which quickly dominates the forest floor by making the soil too acid for other species. Aesthetically, the carpet of sphagnum and its variegated pastel greens contrast with the grey of rock and fallen timber in a harmony of colour; radiant after a rain and the casting of afternoon sun through the lichen curtains. Grey Owl writes:

> Above, below, and on all sides is moss; moss in a carpet,
> deadening the footfall of the traveller, giving beneath

his step, and baffling by its very lack of opposition his efforts to progress. Moss stands in waist-high hummocks, around which detours must be made. Moss in festoons hangs from the dead lower limbs of the trees, like the hangings in some ancient and deserted temple. And a temple it is, raised to the god of silence, of a stillness that so dominates the consciousness that the wanderer who threads its deserted naves treads warily, lest he break unnecessarily a hush that has held sway since time began.

There is whimsical mood to the boreal landscape, a prevailing nervousness — Nature on the edge of change. If challenged, it is quick to temper in unforgiving retribution; its weather and rapids are not to be taken lightly. Grey Owl's connection to the boreal woodland was one of constant ordeal, with the elements, with the government, with regional trappers, and with his personal life and livelihood. The harshness of the land reflected on Owl's character beat him into submission and forced him to change, for the better ... and for a woman's love:

Should the traveller in these solitudes happen to arrive at the edge of one of those high granite cliffs common to the country and look around him, he will see, not the familiar deciduous trees of the south, but will find that he is surrounded, hemmed in on all sides, by apparently endless black forests of spruce, stately trees, cathedral-like with their tall spires above, and their gloomy aisles below. He will see them as far as the eye can reach, covering hill, valley, and ridge, spreading in a green carpet over the face of the earth. Paraded in mass formation, standing stiffly, yet gracefully, to attention, and opposing a wellnigh civilization, until they too shall fall before the axe, a burnt offering on the altar of the God of Mammon.

Ingrid Zschogner.

PART THREE

NATURA

Men argue. Nature acts.
— Voltaire

Like the chapters in a book, or even individual pages within the chapter, the innumerable faces of Nature and Wilderness appear as characters in an unreeling storybook. There are places and events and characters developed, not by a writer's wit and pen, but by the consummate wisdom of a greater power. What you believe to be the greater power is of a personal nature; regardless, the expressive facets of Nature present themselves bereft of any prejudice or favouritism. In a modern world where may be teetering on the brink of environmental catastrophe, we constantly seek the security of absolute truths; an elusive prospect, maybe, but perhaps the absolute truths lay within the primal template of existence, within the natural world that remains untouched; still a stark reminder of how we have despoiled the planet.

15

WHITE PINE

The white pine, king of all the Forest, at one time the mainstay of the lumber industry, is now only existent in a few remote districts, or in reserves set aside by a wise government. But the pine is hard to save. Politics have still a little to say, for it is a profitable tree, and many are the hungry eyes turned on the rolling dark green forest of the reserved lands.

— Grey Owl, *Men of the Last Frontier*

Nearly four centuries ago, the first white explorers — Samuel de Champlain and Étienne Brûlé — accompanied by their Huron guides, plied the waters of the Ottawa River by canoe. They undoubtedly brushed by the seedling trees of the white pine that grew profusely along the shores. Some of these young trees survived the great logging era of the 1800s, several wildfires, harsh winters, and gale-force winds. Scant pockets of white pine old-growth forests have been spared from the modern chainsaw because of their isolation, and more importantly due to the conservation work of Earthroots (formerly known as The Temagami Wilderness Society) and the individuals associated with it.

These trees were already 250 years old by the time of Confederation and the birth of a new country. In 1862, just five years before this event, a white pine was cut down that was over two metres in diameter and sixty-seven metres tall. Timber barons had already arrived on the scene, and every tributary that emptied into the Ottawa River that could float a log became choked with cut pine. Few trees measured less than a metre in thickness at the top, and soon one of the greatest forest genocide operations would denude the valley of its old trees.

When a young Archie Belaney first arrived in Temagami he would have remarked about the wild nature of his surroundings. He may have already seen the desecration of the forests during his train ride north, but Temagami was spared the timberman's axe thanks to the creation of the 5,900-square-mile Temagami Forest Reserve in 1898. Logging never occurred in the heartland of Temagami until Grey Owl had been neatly tucked away in Saskatchewan's Prince Albert National Park in 1930. But the making of the man took place under the shade of the giant white pines that ringed Lake Temagami and dominated the landscape of N'daki Menan — homeland turf of the Teme-Augama Anishnabai.

The skyline of almost every lake and river in Temagami was defined by the rich, thick growth of pine, nearly four hundred trees to the acre, with scarcely another species of tree intermixed among them. The serrated crest of wind-sculpted pine became a hallmark characteristic of Temagami and of the wilderness persona in general. Archie would have camped under the canopy of pine at any number of sites around Bear Island, probably practicing his knife-throwing skills against a dead chicot, or tossing fallen sticks into his campfire. The white pine was a dominant feature in all tourism brochure photographs and written testimonials published by the Temiskaming and Northern Ontario Railway; Daniel O'Connor, local entrepreneur, had founded a steamship company in 1903, as well as constructed three hotels: the Ronnoco in the village; the beautiful Temagami Inn on Temagami Island, built of some of the huge pine cut off the site; and the Lady Evelyn Hotel, located at the north end of the lake.

Belaney arrived in 1907, along with an influx of tourists looking for "soft" adventure. For those arriving by train, for the last hour of their ride, north of North Bay and starting at Tilden Lake, their eyes would rove the landscape, absorbing the grandeur of the forest and the immensity of the trees that towered above them. Tourists would see the pine as a picture-worthy part of the scenery. But to the Anishnabai, the *jingwakoki*, or pinery, was an essential and indispensable facet of their survival and well-being.

The Teme-Augama Anishnabai roots go back almost six thousand years in Temagami. Modern forest "managers" have little cognizance of the importance of the white pine in Canadian cultural significance, but see only the direct commercial value of the wood fibre. *Pinus strobes*, the eastern white pine, is the tallest conifer in eastern Canada and was indoctrinated as Ontario's provincial tree in 1984. Its straight-grained wood, branchless for over half its height, was valued by the British navy for shipbuilding, particularly for one-piece mast construction. For modern timber companies, the wood is sought-after for decorative panelling and beams, square-timber construction, and fine furniture. But for Canada's aboriginal people, the white pine had a different purpose.

Jingwak, the white pine, was valued for its medicinal capabilities, pine nuts or cones as food and decoration, the resin or "sap" as a bonding agent and for its healing qualities, and its stature as a part of their spiritual beliefs. The bodily influence acts primarily as an expectorant; taken from the Latin *expectorare* — "to expel from the chest" — the rendered medicine helps bring up mucus and other material from the lungs, bronchi, and trachea. It reduces the viscosity, or thickness, of bronchial secretions, and thins it enough to be expelled by coughing. Pine nuts or seeds were made into a paste and added to soups and broths; the inner bark was shredded into strips and eaten like spaghetti, or dried and ground into powder to be used as flour. The gum resin, like that of the spruce tree, was chewed like a gum or dried and used as a throat swab for the healing of colds, rheumatism, chronic indigestion, laryngitis, and all chest infections. Heated resin was also used as a dressing to draw out deeply embedded splinters or to heal boils, cuts, and insect stings.

The old-growth forest of pine was also a spiritual landscape to the aboriginal people.

For centuries, nature writers have been writing about human interactions within cultural and aesthetic landscapes as a spiritual journey. Yet the characterization of that journey, or for that matter, the actual archetypal definition of the word *spiritual* as it applies to our explorations within the natural world, remains indefinable. Sure, the pine had tangible physical properties and explainable practical uses, but as a symbol of divine purpose for the Native people is beyond the scope of most of us. The interpretation of Native rock paintings, initially, was incorrectly assessed by white anthropologists as "art" rather than teachings of a spiritual nature. In a cognitive sense, they could only be fully understood by the artist/shaman/teacher who manufactured them. The pine forest as an icon of devout purpose, then, can only be realized by those aboriginals (or others) who worship(ped) the old-growth forest for its life-perpetuating principles.

Gary Potts, chief of the Teme-Augama Anishnabai, had once explained to me that when he stood at the base of a giant pine and touched its trunk, he could "speak" with his ancestors whose bones were in the soil that nurtured the forest. I was told, not that long ago, by an associate sub-chief that, because I was white, I could not find a spiritual connection to the wilderness. Wrong. Within the old-growth pine forest, generally, anyone can enjoy an obvious sense of awe, respect, and wonderment. But how exactly do we interpret the vague feelings of euphoria? How does a non-aboriginal see a tree as an enlightening experience?

The indigenous peoples of North America adapted to the physical landscape soon after the retreat of the great icecaps. Archaic religious characteristics that denoted a symbiotic relationship with the cycle of Nature were already prevalent. First Peoples believed in the animate qualities of all things. Survival as individuals, and within community social structures, depended on controlling and manipulating cosmic, spiritual powers within the Natural World. The great pine forests of eastern Canada were an integral part of their very existence.

Spirituality then, perhaps, understands an ecosystem from a culturally explicit, primitive way — the energy of the *cycle of life* in which humans are only one part. Traditional western practices, in dealing with forest or wilderness management, negate the spiritual inferences by concentrating on the "separateness" or disconnected importance of wild lands, trees, et cetera, and opting for a strictly monetary evaluation. This is a self-indulgent, human-centred, linear approach to understanding our Native cultures, and one more reason why forest managers believe that a fragmented forest ecosystem can survive in a fractured, separate state.

Non-economic values have always been hard to define. When eco-warriors first began their defiant and valiant stand to protect ancient pine forests, it was an emotional, philosophical, and spiritual plea; hardly the weapons needed to combat the quick-fire, tangible economic force of industry. Spiritually, one needs only to closely examine, understand, and absorb the fundamental cultural values of the forest ecosystem, not in a scientific or even rational way, but as a place of "beginning" ... maybe as a template of all life on this planet. Protecting spiritual values cannot be isolated to a single tree, or even a forest stand; rather a broader approach to connecting whole ecosystems and all their supporting values. The most difficult task ahead is to do the impossible — to sensitize forest managers to spiritual values even when we cannot define them in logical terms.

The giant white pine has played an important role in my own life. It was the largest tree on our property when I was growing up. In its branches I could get lost, be comforted, feel and see the world around me from its lofty perspective; later, as an aesthetic elixir, the pine-forest landscape symbolized the raw, artistic nature of wilderness. Finally, it became a subjective reason to change forest mismanagement through environmental action. My own spiritual connection with *jingwakoki* evolved through all of this, somewhat inconspicuously over years of close association.

Travelling by primitive ways through the wilderness and spending nights out under the pines, for years, has allowed me to enjoy the more recondite pleasures of the ancient forest. There is a music played by the wind through the needles of the white pine, singular, different from the coarseness of the red or Jack pine, or other conifers; a softer, melodic, almost ghostly composition that surges and swells in the gusts. A lullaby.

What a shame if, when all the white pines have disappeared, the music will end, and the spirits will no longer have a conduit to speak to the living.

Grey Owl, in "The Land of Shadows," glimpsed this possibility:

> Not much longer can the forest hope to stem the tide of progress; change is on every hand. Every year those who follow the receding Border further and further back, see one by one the links with the old days being severed,

as the demands of a teeming civilization reach tentacles into the very heart of the Wild Lands. And we who stand regretfully and watch, must either adapt ourselves to the new conditions, or, preferably, follow the ever-thinning line of last defence into the shadows, where soon will vanish every last one of the Dwellers amongst the Leaves.

16

STORMS

The Height of Land is, for some reason, the breeding place
of storms of a severity and suddenness that makes a famil-
iarity with the signs preceding them imperative to those
itineraries include lakes of any size.
　　　　　— Grey Owl, *Men of the Last Frontier*, "The Trail"

It was just one of those days. It was just one of those guided trips where
everything went right. I hadn't forgotten anything, like toilet paper, or cutlery, or tent poles; the food was cooked just right, the clients — three small
children and amiable parents — all melded into canoe trip routines with
uncanny perfection. It was a perfect route, too: a climb up Maple Mountain,
taking pictures of moose feeding in the shallows, easy lakes, level portages,
copious blueberries, and perfect weather. I had even taken the kids away
from the parents for an afternoon, to swim on a secret beach on an island
away from our campsite, as if castaways on a shipwreck adventure and we
were the only ones in the world — a lost paradise. A rogue storm cloud
made its quick appearance: flipping over the canoe, we sat out a ten-min-
ute shower and brief display of lightning, sitting under the boat and eating
peanut butter sandwiches. The sun came out and it was a perfect afternoon.

"Is that all Temagami can throw at us?" remarked the father when we
returned. Laughter. The kids looked north across the lake, at the island
paradise, and taunted the forces of Nature to *do better than that!*

"Be careful what you wish for," I told them. More laughter … except I wasn't joining in on the amusement. The trip wasn't over yet.

The next day was different. I was pretty good at predicting weather patterns, and it was still several years before climate change fucked things up. Patterns that were easy to read: cloud formations, sundogs, halo's around the moon, *rain before seven clears by eleven* — blueprints for what was to come — were all there, making my job simpler, and the clients would think you were some kind of soothsayer and they would ask, "how did you know that it was going to rain?" It was magic.

Well, the magic was about to turn into a sorcerer's nightmare. We paddled only a short distance that day and made camp on a leeside point just before the main body of Diamond Lake. There was a slight warm breeze out of the southwest and clouds had been building all after-noon. Tents were pitched and the kids went for a swim while the parents watched. I felt uneasy about the relative calm; the air was heavy and the wind came in sporadic gusts. No birds sang.

While the family was engaged down by the water, I walked to the rise above the camp so I could look out over the lake in the direction of the weather. The wind was noticeably stronger here and the lake was starting to show some chop, but what struck me numb was the intensity of the clouds over the near horizon. It was more than the typical anvil-shaped cumulonimbus thunderhead approaching at breakneck speed; it was a supercell microburst, or what we called a "push" storm. In other words, there was a ground tornado set to hit our campsite in about ten minutes.

Be careful what you wish for.

In "The Trail," Grey Owl warns, "In a country of this description it is well to pitch camp, even if only for a night, with due regard for possible fall-ing timber or cloud-bursts; in dealing with the unsleeping, subtle Enemy, ready to take advantage of the last error, it is well to overlook nothing."

Ten minutes was all the time I had to figure out what to do. And what does one do in these situations when there is no place to go. I ran down to the campsite and threw up a quick rain tarp in a stand of small trees and placed extra tent pegs in the tents and strung extra guy-lines to nearby trees. The parents wondered what was going on and asked what they should do.

"We can just wait it out in the tents," the father said.

"No, no tents, it's too dangerous, we'll stand under the tarp I put up," I informed the parents in a somewhat protracted composed tone. They had no idea.

"The fierce rattle of the rain on the feeble shelter, the howling of the wind, the splintering crash of falling trees, which, should one fall on the tent, would crush every soul within it ..." wrote Grey Owl in "The Trail."

The kids thought it was just a game. From our position, being somewhat protected from the approaching storm, all the prep-work seemed a little melodramatic to the family; after all, the storm yesterday was a paltry excuse for Mother Nature's wrath.

I had just enough time to tether the two canoes to a tree before it struck.

"There's canoes out on the lake," one of the kids shouted. Sure enough, a party of six canoes were out in the middle of the channel, about to be hit with galeforce winds. When they suddenly realized the intensity of the storm about to descend on them, they turned toward the far shore of the bay, almost half a kilometre away. The wind hit with such a force it was impossible to walk erect without gripping for a hand-hold. We were under the tarp when the rain came, but we were missing one of the kids. The mother shouted and an eight-year-old came running out of the tent just as a tree came crashing down beside it. The wind picked the youth up and spun him in circles across the campsite and halfway to the lake. I bolted at the same time and grabbed the boy, dragged him back to the rain tarp, and pressed two of the smallest kids up against the trunk of a tree and held them there. The tarp did nothing to protect us from the rain; all we could do was to wait and hope the storm didn't get any worse. The family was terrified but stoic, the children wide-eyed and shivering but respectfully in awe of the maelstrom unfolding around them.

The six canoes had capsized as soon as the storm hit. Waves a metre high were too much for their skill level to mitigate, and they were all forced to swim ashore. By the time they washed onto the beach, the storm had passed and the sun had broken through the remnant clouds.

The family was shaken up but intact and thankful that they got off as easy as they did. It could have been much worse.

There is something exquisite and ultimately supernatural about big storms, and like anything explainable in scientific jargon and absolute reasoning, the magic is still there; *Nature possessed*, in its ostentatious character, brazen and all-powerful. And while few ever get the opportunity to allow themselves the privilege of a close encounter, unplugged from the safe confines of urban existence, those who venture off the beaten path in the remnant wilderness we have left have had a brush with the big storm.

The feeling of powerlessness and uncertainty is what defines a particular facet of the adventure experience. There is ultimately an excitement in the *not* knowing what's around the next corner. Granted, we can manage the risk factor, somewhat, by employing age-old preparation tactics (like not standing under the biggest tree during a thunder storm), but there are times, though, when you can do nothing at all but hope.

During the three hundred or more expeditions I have been on, there have been many instances where little protection is afforded, particularly in the Far North tundra or on the larger Shield rivers whose banks are too precipitous to climb, and where you are forced to find whatever shelter you can along gravel flats or sandbars.

On one such trip, while paddling with friends, along with my two children (ages two and four at the time) on Ontario's Albany River, there were few places to camp except on the wide gravel bars. The day was humid, and by afternoon a large supercell had formed in the southwest and was moving quickly in our direction. Just how quickly a storm like this can move is critical in the timing of procuring shelter, and this time I had my two children to think of. I concluded that we had no more than fifteen minutes to get under cover, so I made the call for the four canoes to beach on river left, along a sandy spit of land that had a slight rise but no vegetation at all. We carried the gear across the spit and literally dragged the canoes over the sand without taking out the miscellaneous small stuff that accumulates during the day, and over the rise to a low spot that afforded some protection from the expected wind. We flipped over the canoes and stacked them tight on top of the packs. Managing to pitch two of the low-profile dome tents,[8] all but my two-year-old daughter and myself made it to the safety of shelter before the storm hit.

Thinking I had enough time to pitch the larger screen-tent, and believing that it would actually stay up in a high wind, was a bad call on my part. This type of shelter is only wind-worthy if tied out securely, double-roped, and to unyielding objects like rocks or trees. Here there was just sand and cobblestone. My daughter was inside, sitting on the wannigan,[9] when the wind hit with the force of a tornado; anything not securely pinioned blew off the spit like tissue paper — life jackets, fanny packs, whitewater helmets — airborne, dropping helter-skelter out in the lagoon beyond our camp.

"Papa, are we okay?" shouted a little voice from inside. I had a death-grip on the windward support pole of the shelter while the bulk of it trailed off into the sky, the remaining poles bending and warping like pipe-cleaners under the force of the wind. My little girl was in a pocket of safety so long as I could keep a tight grip on the shelter to prevent it from completely flying off. In as calm a voice as I could muster, I assured my daughter that this would be over soon. I felt everything lifting slightly and I realized the nylon shelter was billowing like a sail, and if I didn't secure my footing, I would soon be hang-gliding over the Albany River. Luckily, my daughter was sitting on the wannigan, which had pinched some of the shelter fabric to the ground, helping to keep it from taking off like a kite.

---

8   Some tents are better than others in heavy winds; the dome tent, because of its shape, can withstand winds of up to seventy-five kilometres per hour or more if securely pinioned to the ground. Traditional A-frame tents are practical only when there is ample cover from high winds, making the dome-style tent the preferred choice with adventurers in the Far North.

9   A wannigan is a traditional box used to carry camp goods and kitchen gear, and carried by way of a twenty-two-inch leather tump strap, looped around so one can carry it on their back, suspended by a wider headband.

Ten minutes is a long time to battle the ferocity of gale-force winds and pelting rain; it can be interminably long if you're unprepared. I was prepared, to a point, but caught short by the speed of the storm. And it is sometimes difficult to estimate just how much time you have in order to get off the water and secure your camp; line-of-sight (visual reference points and proximity to horizon) plays an important role in this calculation.

There have been many occasions on my travels in the backcountry, mostly when I was with the Park Service, when I would race a storm to the end of a lake. And more times than not, it wouldn't just be a casual cloudburst, but an out-and-out tempest of proportionate size.

One time, within several hundred metres of the shore, where the intention was to hastily flip over the canoe and lay beneath until the storm had passed, our progress in the canoe was such that we knew it may not be possible to make it without the help of the gods. Generally, a great gust of wind precedes the storm; this particular incident was different, though, in that it remained eerily calm while the thick, black clouds consumed the entire sky around us. I could sense something moving in behind my partner and I, who were by this time paddling as if our lives depended on it. There was a hissing noise followed by several abrupt gusts and a quick shower of ice pellets. Since the wind was behind us, we had thought we could take advantage of the leverage and began paddling even harder. The shore, by this time, was a mere half-kilometre away and it looked as if we were in the clear. I've handled a canoe in just about every situation; intentionally planned-out expeditions traversing lakes that take three days to cross, and riding miles upon miles of seething whitewater through canoe-devouring boulder gardens; however, there are events and things in Nature that occasionally surface that transcend all the inherent skills you have learned and the knowledge acquired to mitigate them successfully.

Behind us and nearly upon us was a water spout, pressed to the lake by clouds so dense they resembled black volcanic rocks pouring in a wave across the lake. Even though the spout veered and faded, we were hit by such a force of wind to be practically lifted above the water, and it was all I could do to keep the paddle firmly planted as a rudder, desperate to keep the canoe pointing forward. Paddling was abandoned and exchanged with high braces in order to manage the breaking waves we were now surfing, water slipping into the bow and stern at every dip and rise of the canoe. Rain pelted down, mixed with pebble-size hail that created a solid white curtain between us and the shore. Managing to steer the canoe into a tight gravel beach, we both jumped out into the water and hauled up our gear, which by now was totally soaked. A lightning strike exploded no more than fifty metres away in a concave bay to our right. It had targeted a large white pine, the top of which was now totally gone; splintered shards littered the bay almost a hundred metres out into the lake.

Tucking what we could of our gear up into available spaces, we curled up under the canoe and waited. And as it is the nature of most northern storms of violent temperament, they are over quickly, within minutes; but the damage they can mete out is terrific and terrible. No sooner had we settled under the canoe than the storm had drifted off and the sun was already probing for space in the scattering clouds. Smoke was filtering up through the shore pines and, upon closer inspection, we found that the tree that had been struck by lightning was smouldering at the base. A white pine has shallow roots that trail along the surface of underlying rock, tendrils gripping in and onto any crack available. The lightning blast had followed the expansive root system, literally blowing it apart, and it was now smouldering. Not yet a full-fledged fire, as is so often the case with lightning-caused boreal wildfires, we were able to douse it easily with water from the lake.

Grey Owl, in "The Trail," describes how he had "seen masses of water the height of a pine tree and ten yards across, spiralling and spinning across the center of lakes at terrific speed in the spring of the year. With them a canoe has little chance. I once saw a point of heavy timber, perhaps thirty acres in extent, whipped, and lashed, and torn into nothing but a pile of roots and broken tree-stumps, in the space of fifteen seconds."

Some storms in the Far North have yet a different disposition and obstinacy that wears thin the veil of patience and prudence. The hardest thing for most modern travellers is to stay in one location for more than a day. While on a client trip a few summers ago, we were forced to evacuate the Thelon River at Warden's Grove. Our ten-person group was flown south to a headwaters eco-lodge to wait out a violent windstorm hailing from the Baker Lake region. After a few days of hiking the tundra sand eskers and hummock flats, we were able to once again proceed on our canoe trip, but from a location that necessitated travel over tundra lakes. Since these lakes are always shallow, with little wind cover, it doesn't take much of a breeze to whip up waves and to make travel impossible.

Two days into our second attempt, the wind did come up and forced us onto an island in the middle of Lynx Lake — a relatively small lake but large enough to effectually shut us down. With the wind came a steady barrage of rain and sleet for almost three days. The tents were pitched in a hollow, slightly protected from the wind by a small esker. It is in this situation that the actual storm and its various components is more easily tolerated than having to manage and massage the needs of various clients who require constant entertaining. A guide only has so many tricks up his sleeve, and being isolated on a small island, possibly two hundred metres in diameter, things do become repetitious and banal. If it weren't for the company of Kirk Wipper — good friend and mentor and the founding father of the Canadian Canoe Museum — and his eternal collection of worldly anecdotes, stories, and tall tales, we would have had to suffer through my trifling repertoire of harmonica tunes.

It is no surprise that I enjoy a good storm. It is Nature at its most animated state; just raw, unadulterated energy. The wind stirs something primitive in the soul and shakes the very inner fibres of your being.

> *Oh that my tongue were in the thunder's mouth!*
> *Then with a passion would I shake the world.*[10]

Over the years I have found myself in strange places and predicaments, having to deal with the worst of storms or, more aptly, *the best of storms*. To love storms is to embrace Nature on its terms, not yours, and to learn to relax into a state of consciousness that manages fear. Not always an easy or sure thing to master.

---

10   From Shakespeare's *King John*, Act 3, Scene 4.

I offered to act as a second mate on a sailing trip with a client of mine who was a sailing instructor from Long Island, New York. The destination was Chesapeake Bay, and we had rented a thirty-two-foot sloop from the anchorage at Annapolis. It was late October and weather was unpredictable; a hurricane was brewing off the Florida coast and we were keeping a close watch on its movements. After sailing in stiff winds for two days, the small-craft warning was issued, but we decided to keep to our scheduled plan regardless. We were currently on the west side of the bay, just north of Smith Point Light, with plans to cross the fifty-mile stretch east to Chincoteague Bay and Tobacco Island, a few kilometres north of Accomack. There was a sheltered bay and anchorage there, but we were more interested in the revered clam and oyster bar — famous landmark on the east shore of the Chesapeake.

Winds were out of the southeast at over seventy knots and expected to increase later that day. We ran for the first hour under full sail but that proved to be too much torque on the mast, with the boat already keeled over, running at an even forty-five-degree angle. Balancing the force of the sails against the drag of the keel, we managed to align the boat in such a way to keep it pointing into the wind, avoiding broaching the waves that were rolling at about four to six metres. After the mainsail was dropped, we kept up a storm sail with the jib alone, which was enough to keep a steady track across the bay.

I had sailed many times with canoes lashed together, using a jury-rigged square sail that had serious limitations if the wind was hailing from any direction other than on the tail. Here, we were deep-keeled and rigged for running into the wind at more than ten knots, which was working like a charm. Handling the boat on the swells took some getting used to, but I soon found a comfortable rhythm, managing it like I would if I were canoeing across breaking waves on a large lake. I could feel each wave, each crest surge and the vertigo of dropping into the trough, over again and again, the wheel spinning on the drop and a quick grasp to pull it around on the rise up. All the while the rain pelted us, and for hours we held our course to the Tobacco Islands; at times we were heeled over far enough for the port rails to submerge. There were no other boats anywhere.

When we pulled into the anchorage we were greeted by the curious and the critical. Everyone else had pulled into port the day before and had long since been indulged with wine and crabmeat. They questioned why we were out on the bay in such weather and told us it seemed too dangerous to sail across in the face of a hurricane. Our answer was succinct and honest. "We came to sail, and that's what we did," is all we said.

Winter storms are different, and I've been in enough of them while winter tripping to know that simple procedures can turn into death-defying tribulations. Again, I learned that it is far wiser to stay put than to give in to the urge to break camp and move on or to keep to some prescribed schedule. Time? Why leave a perfectly comfortable camp for the singular purpose of making time, especially when you know that a storm looms and that travel will be compromised anyway. I've made mistakes, as did Grey Owl; making assumptions on the day's upcoming labours and ignoring both the immutable set patterns in the weather and your sense of better judgment.

As Grey Owl warns, in "The Land of Shadows":

> A rise in temperature often precipitates a blizzard, and these winter storms are so violent as to destroy whole areas of timber by sheer weight alone; the solitary trapper caught on the trail by one of these tempests, with little or no warning, especially if crossing any large lake, is in grave danger. His dogs blinded and half-choked by the wind-driven masses of snow cannot face the storm. Himself unable to break trail through the mounting drifts, or to keep his direction through the whirling white wall that surrounds him at the distance of a few feet, he may, if far from land, perish miserably.

17

THE PURE SPRING

The craving for something cold is paramount. You've been paddling for several hours in the sweltering heat and the filtered water from the lake you've been drinking for the past two weeks is tepid and flat. You dread the long portage coming up but remember the water spring you found last trip through, about two-thirds of the way across. It's now even too hot for the blackflies and mosquitoes and they've let up until the cool of the evening.

You shoulder your pack — the lighter one — and hoist the canoe over your head and trudge uphill the first two hundred metres to where the trail tracks off onto level ground, for a while anyway, before it dips over a rock knob and plains out again into a morass of beaver grass and tamarack. Gravity pulls your load down and the pack straps bite into your shoulders; the canoe thwart eats away at your neck and shoulder muscles and after a thousand metres you begin to cringe at every hard step. Sweat drips off the end of your nose in a steady flow; you begin to curse the day, the portage, God, your ex-wife. Just a few steps farther. And there it is — the pure spring, just like last time, gurgling and sputtering out of the ground, born out of the earth and shaded by pines.

You literally drop your load at the side of the trail, kneel beside the spring, cup your hands and dip them in the water. The water feels particularly cold, and you bring it to your mouth quickly to enjoy the sensation in its fullest. The water is almost sweet, like maple sap in the spring, with a slight earthy, iron taste. You feel life easing back into your limbs and the ache in your neck subsides and all your immediate cares diminish as the spring water takes effect like morphine. You refill your water bottle but lament the fact that the water will lose its coolness quickly in this heat so you stow it deep inside your pack. The coolness of the shade is intoxicating as you stretch out over the moss and pine needles; even the air has a different texture to it — moister, richer, fragrant with the aroma of deep forest. You leave refreshed, both in body and spirit, and the trail no longer seems as difficult.

Water ... we need it, we waste it, we despoil it, and we take it for granted; and clean water is getting scarce. The Worldwatch Institute (WWI) has called water scarcity "the most underappreciated global environmental challenge of our time."

And why is that? Probably because we North Americans still live and thrive in a water-rich environment; what we don't know, though, is the nature of the water we choose to ingest — where it comes from, and what's in it that might potentially harm us.

In the outdoor trade, where market trends drive the industry, the use of reusable polycarbonate bottles such as those made by Nalgene and Camelbak were touted as a necessary part of the accoutrement. I remember teaching winter wilderness skills to students for Outward Bound, where water was boiled and then put into plastic Nalgene bottles to be used as a hot water bottle to warm sleeping bags; and because the water wouldn't freeze, it could be consumed the next day.

The problem, as it turned out, was the fact that polycarbonates contain the endocrine-disrupting chemical bisphenol-A (BPA), which can leak into the liquids they contain. BPA mimics the female hormone estrogen and is a known carcinogen. BPA has been linked to breast and prostate cancers and is assumed to play a role in the development of Alzheimer's disease and even diabetes. And it gets worse. When you heat liquids in poly-bottles (baby bottles in a microwave for instance), BPAs flood into the contents, creating a toxic cocktail. So, for all those health-oriented outdoor enthusiasts taking to the backcountry in the hopes of enjoying a healthy adventure, it may have been a wiser choice to dip your cup directly into the stream and take your chance at contracting giardiasis than pumping and filtering your water into a toxic bottle. Nalgene and Camelbak are now touting BPA- and phthalate-free bottles made by Eastman using the new plastic polymer "Tritan copolyester." Tests yet are not conclusive as to the actual health benefits (or hazards) of the new material.

Although a serious concern, I find it tragically amusing to watch how different trends that are supposedly created to offer us a higher quality of life actually harm us. Health, well-being, convenience, and status are common New Age pursuits; the environment is also a consideration for a lot of people, and that's caused a huge cultural shift and an infatuation with bottled water. Perrier bottled water has been an iconic status symbol, and it is even purported that Michael Jackson bathed in the stuff, while Madonna simulated oral sex with an Evian bottle in her 1991 documentary *Truth or Dare.*

Bottled water became a faddish symbol of crass conspicuous consumer madness. The mystique of mineral water from springs "untouched-by-man" sparked an increase of sales in the millions of bottles. With the advent of the go-anywhere plastic bottles made of polyethylene terephthalate or PET, bottled water sales in the United States rose from 115 million in 1990 to four billion bottles in 1997. Today, worldwide, sales top two hundred billion bottles sold each year at a price tag of nearly nine billion dollars.

Our addiction to water quality is, and ironically so, making us sicker. There is new evidence that the phthalates in flexible plastics interfere with our endocrine system.

Aside from personal health issues, there is the serious impact on the environment. Two million tons of empty bottles hit landfill sites every year. Our idealization of water bubbling out of mountains has led to mountains of un-recycled crap. According to the Container Recycling Institute (CRI), less than 15 percent of PET products are recycled; that means a much heavier dependency on new materials for production. The Earth Policy Institute (EPI) estimates that it takes more than seventeen million barrels of oil to make enough PET bottles to meet America's demand — that's enough fuel to power one million cars for an entire year. And then there are the shipping costs. It's a huge carbon footprint. And what's the deal with bottled water anyway; Pepsi and Coca-Cola, who got in on the action, producing their popular Aquafina and Dasani brands, derive their product from municipal water systems ... and that's another subject of criticism. Just how safe is the water coming out of our taps? Well, not very.

Antiquated lead-soldered pipes and filtering systems fail to remove twenty-first-century contaminates such as pesticides, industrial chemicals, and arsenic. City water systems add chlorine or chloramine as a disinfectant to kill certain bacteria. But chlorine is only good until we drink it. Chlorine upsets the natural bacterial balance in the body; even showering with chlorinated water is harmful over time — the chlorine-laden mist is ingested into the lungs and the dilated pores of the skin. Chlorine use in the early part of the twentieth century was introduced into water systems to curb the spread of cholera and typhoid epidemics. It worked. Instead, though, people started dying of long-term chronic digestive diseases, cancer, and arteriosclerosis.

And then there's the question of fluoride in public water systems. Touted by the national health agencies and dental fraternity as a necessary component to help reduce tooth decay, the use of fluoride in municipal water supplies has a chequered history of cover-up and mass brainwashing. Benefits in prevention are now questionable, compared with the cumulative negative effects over time. The effect is hardest on young boys with growing bones: bones absorb half of the fluoride and its use is now linked to bone cancers — the same cancer that killed Canadian icon Terry Fox. Also suspected are neurological disorders, reduced intelligence, and impaired thyroid function. At least kids are dying with good teeth.

The classic fringe movement movie *Dr. Strangelove*, in which a demented United States general fears that fluoridation was a communist plot, wasn't far off the mark. I asked a client of mine, Dr. Paul Lepor, a general practitioner who turned to alternative treatments with great success in the Midwest states, if fluoride in drinking water was a good thing.

"Absolutely not," he replied with an obvious fury.

"It's a byproduct from the nuclear bomb days," he explained. "Stuff left over they didn't know what to with so they put it in drinking water."

During the 1940s and 50s, fluoride was needed to enrich uranium as part of the nuclear weapons program, or what was known as the Manhattan Project. One of the world's largest industrial buildings was the Fluoride Gaseous Diffusion Plant in Tennessee. The waste product was deemed harmful to workers, so studies were concealed and excuses fabricated to tout fluoride as a tooth-decay preventative. This was all done to prevent any lawsuits from factory workers. This is the same scientific fraternity that peddled the benefits of lead in gasoline. Today, most of the fluoride comes from raw industrial waste scrubbed from the smokestacks at Florida's phosphate plants.

Oddly enough, Health Canada and the Canadian Dental Association still maintain the validity of fluoride in tap water. Almost half the population in Canada live in communities still using fluoridated water (exceptions are British Columbia and Quebec). Other than Australia, North America contains the only group of countries in the world using fluoride in their public watering holes. The only way to remove fluoride from tap water is through reverse osmosis or distillation. Bottled water … or tap water? If either chlorine or fluoride was introduced into the healthcare system today, they wouldn't meet industry or consumer safety standards. So, doesn't it make sense to fix the problem with our tap water instead of flogging bottled water?

"*C'mon, shaganash, lighten up,*" Archie barked.

"*What are you talking about, Owl? People should know the truth,*" I said.

"*The truth? People don't care about the truth unless they trip over it and it's in their way.*"

"*Yeah, right, then they just shove it under the carpet and forget about it. Anyway, Owl, what do you know about water quality; you still lived during a time when you could dip your pannikan over the gunnel of your canoe into any lake wherever you paddled and have good clean water to drink. It wasn't an issue then, and you rarely mention water quality at all in any of your books!*"

"*Good point, shaganash. Still, people can't see the forest for the trees,*" Archie answered.

"*Yeah, and most of the trees have been cut down, don't forget, Archie.*" Owl was gearing up for a monologue.

"*In my days,*" Owl began, "*it was incomprehensible that water would be an issue in the Great Beyond. The rich rewards of the forest, yes, went to the lumberman, and the minerals to the miner, but the great flooding of lands from these power dams that I have seen in your world have laid waste to Indian Lands and made the water brackish and bitter.*"

You have no idea, Owl, what you're missing.

18

ICE WALKER

The ice was on its last legs and the snow soft and mushy,
making hard going, And about ten miles from camp I was
obliged to cache everything, and taking only a few traps
and a light axe, high-banked it around the lake shores,
getting in not long before dawn after some very precarious
bouts with bad ice.

— Grey Owl, *Tales of an Empty Cabin*, "On Hardship"

I was twelve years old when I witnessed two people fall through the ice. They were people I knew well — my older brother and younger cousin. It was a terrifying experience, albeit more for them because they were the ones foolish enough to walk on thin ice. I had a bad feeling about the conditions, even though the air temperature was at least minus 30 Celsius, they were walking near a beaver dam outlet on a small lake. Not that I had more experience than they did at recognizing poor ice conditions, it was more of a sixth sense or gut feeling that saved my ass. I fell back behind them, saying that I didn't feel that it was a good way to go; it didn't *feel* safe. They laughed and plodded on, leaving me behind. Then they fell through the ice.

Luckily, it was shallow enough and they hit bottom waist deep and managed to pull themselves out quickly. But in that temperature the

water froze instantly on their clothing, like armour, stiffening quickly, making it all the more difficult to walk the two miles back to the house. My cousin was crying and my brother and I urged him on, to keep moving as fast as we could. Those two miles along the pipeline right-of-way and back to my cousins' house seemed to take forever, the late afternoon temperature plunging steadily as the sun dropped to the horizon. My uncle was furious, to say the least, and he threw the two of them into a steaming hot bath that would have cooked a chicken. I remember the screams; and the more they screamed, the harder the lecture from my uncle. I was given a hot chocolate and a hug.

I was lucky. It's sometimes difficult to gauge the thickness of the ice beneath your feet; there are so many variables and peculiarities with ice that continually prompt your sense of judgment.

Old Archie Payne, who had been driving his car over the same ice for almost half a century on Lake Rosseau in Muskoka, had no reason to think things would ever be different. But with changing climate patterns, the ice didn't take on its normal rigidity; Archie's car went through the ice and he drowned. He was ninety-four years old.

And he's not alone; every winter people go through the ice, people who should know better, or people who know better but some quirk in Nature beguiled their better sense of caution. Snowmobilers often go through the ice because they have this false sense of security, thinking that if they keep moving they can stay on top of any ice; but in most cases, machines get bogged down in deep slush, lose their forward momentum, and then fall through.

Last winter, a mother and her twelve-year-old daughter went through the ice at a pressure crack using the exact same trail they had passed only two hours before. They were riding an All Terrain Vehicle and had secured themselves in by using the seat-belt harnesses. The father/husband was riding a snow machine behind them, and when he witnessed his family dropping through the ice, he jumped off his skidoo and screamed for them to take off their seat belts. But in the mayhem, his wife and daughter were unable to unfasten themselves and he watched in horror as the ice closed in behind them and they dropped forty feet to the bottom of the lake.

The first thing I had learned about travelling on lake ice in a vehicle was not to wear your seatbelt, and to drive with a window down just in case you do go through the ice. Even so, the times I did drive on the ice on Lake Temagami I had lost all sense of "touch" with the environment. I felt vulnerable and fearful, even though I knew the ice to be thirty inches thick, and solid enough to support the weight of a fully loaded transport truck. When homesteading in Mattawa and living on the shore of the Ottawa River — a river that had captured the souls of many an unfortunate log driver, I was informed by a Snake Creek old-timer that they used to drive a team of horses over the river on just two inches of steel ice. No thanks. Two inches of ice isn't enough of a security blanket to rely on.

One winter, just before Christmas, the ice thickened enough on Lake Temagami to drive my jeep on it without too much concern, at least out to an island lodge where I was staying while designing a ski trail on Temagami Island. The weather was intense, turning from pleasant to tempestuous in a matter of hours. Two inches of rain fell overnight and the wind knocked out power to the islands.

The lodge owner feared that his water lines would freeze if he didn't get to town to pick up a generator he had purchased. I said I'd get across the lake in my jeep and drive the twenty-five kilometres to town as a favour for letting me stay at the lodge for free. It was a distance of about one kilometre to the mainland from the lodge; not that far to drive if the conditions were good, over an ice road that was normally well-maintained. But now it was under water. There was so much rain that the weight of it pushed the lake ice down and the wind was tossing up whitecaps as if there was no ice at all. It was discomforting to drive over deep water on ice that may not even be there, and as I proceeded slowly, doors taken off my jeep just in case, I could feel myself sinking slowly into oblivion. What made it worse was the fact that it was night time.

Water started spilling in through the door openings and covering my headlights, yet I was still sinking down and not really knowing if I'd just slip right off the ice shelf altogether. Then, slowly, nearing the mainland, I felt my jeep rising up out of the depths. My heart was pounding so hard I had to pull over and catch my breath before driving to town over icy roads. I had to retrace my path on my return, but at least I knew the jeep would make it back.

Others weren't so lucky. Night temperatures dropped severely, freezing the lake water around vehicles whose engines had cut out, stranding their passengers until they could be rescued. It was a strange sight, looking at cars frozen into the lake up to their windshields; older vehicles left to fall through the ice during the spring melt, or newer ones that would have to be physically chipped and chainsawed out.

As a young adventurer, it took me years to gain a comfortable knowledge of ice conditions and winter travel techniques. I had certainly honed some skill at summer canoe travel but I quickly learned that techniques employed in balmy, polite weather, don't apply at all in the winter. Simple tasks, like collecting firewood, for example, or making a fire, could be life-threatening ordeals; in the least, putting you in some peril of injury or extreme discomfort.

I was seventeen when I embarked on my first *real* winter expedition. Driving north with a friend, we intended to camp out along the Highland Hiking Trail in Algonquin Provincial Park. Not a great distance north but enough to notice that the skiff of snow covering the ground at home north of Toronto was now nearly a metre deep in the hills of Algonquin. After parking the car, we trekked about five kilometres along the trail by snowshoe in the winter paradise until we came to a clearing — a prospective spot for a campsite.

Normally, while ski touring, or winter camping, a tent site could easily be packed down and left to sinter (harden) so that the tent could be pitched above the smooth, deep snow pack. Not knowing this, my friend and I began shovelling out a hole for the tent with our snowshoes as shovels; a rather Herculean task just to reach bare ground that turned out to be infested with rocks, fallen logs, and alder shrubs — all the things invisible to the eye, but buried deep under the snow. It took an inordinate amount of valuable time to clear a site that was really unfit for a tent, the ridgepole barely at the level of the surrounding snow surface, and having to climb down into a hole to get in or out of the tent. We thought it was brilliant at the time, though, because it afforded us more protection from the wind.

Now it was time to dig a firepit. This required another excavation of proportion, enough to build a safe fire and to sit around it comfortably. Later I learned that a fire could be built over a packed snow base using a raft of logs for support. But I was destined to find out how to do things in the outdoors the hard way.

Collecting firewood was another matter. There was a surfeit of dead, standing trees, or chicots, that would provide enough firewood for the few days we would base camp there. No problem. Taking out my axe, I approached the nearest chicot and took a swing at it in earnest; and I say earnest because it was getting late now and we were both getting cold from the sweat produced during the heavy toil of digging two large holes in the snow. After the second chop, I was knocked unconscious. The reverberation of hitting a dead tree two metres above its solid base with the axe caused the top of the tree to break off and come crashing down on my head. Thankfully, when I came to, my friend had not witnessed what I had done. He had gone out with his axe to get firewood nearby; when I got to him he was sitting on the ground, rubbing his head, a chunk of tree lying beside him.

"Be careful," he said. "Watch the top doesn't break off and hit you in the head."

"What, do you think I'm stupid," I answered jokingly. More digging. We didn't bring a saw with us, which would have been the smart thing to do, so we shovelled around the base of a few trees so we could fell them without fear of the tops breaking off. Once we had a decent pile of wood collected, a fire was lit in the smoke-pit. And smoky it was: since the fire was trying to burn below surface level, there was absolutely no draft to keep it lit. Smoke hung in a thick pall in the hole we had dug, stinging our eyes and making it difficult to cook dinner. Yet, neither of us complained; the spirit of the adventure overrode any of the more unpleasant situations. *This is the way you do it,* I pondered with a measure of doubt.

We still needed water. To get water all you had to do was melt snow; and this we did for the first day, but it takes a lot of work to get enough to make tea … and snow tea is mildly unpleasant, especially if the snow is taken from the edge of a swamp — it has this rusty nail, methane flavour with a hue of tree bark. It was decided that we would chop a hole in the pond ice. Another simple task if you had brought along an ice auger; but to chop a hole through ice in late winter requires a particular skill and a lot of axe-work. Here the ice was almost three feet thick, and to reach water at that thickness required we chop a hole about four feet in diameter. Even at that, it took over an hour and one broken axe handle to punch through to water. The tea still tasted like swamp.

Knowing when and on what ice to travel over safely is a bit of an acquired talent. Blended with a share of gut feeling and brazen luck, hard science of water in its solid state still has this mystic quality to it. Nature is full of inconsistencies. Just ask old Archie. Even steadfast trails over lake and river ice, used for weeks, can weaken and shift, from currents below, heat from subsurface objects, and even the refraction of sunlight can change the consistency and rigidity of ice long before the spring melt.

My wife fell through the ice while skiing up at my cabin on the Lady Evelyn, the winter we stayed with our two babies and filed stories for Citytv in Toronto. It was a well-used trail along the shore of the river; I had hauled hundreds of pounds of firewood along the trail and there were no signs of weak ice. She had our daughter in a carrier on her back, stepped only inches off the main trail to avoid skiing into a cabin guest, Kirk Wipper, who had stopped to adjust his ski poles, and she went through up to her waist. The infant carrier seemed to suspend her from going any deeper, and old Kirk gallantly helped her out. I was ahead, pulling my son in the pulk, and was oblivious to what had just transpired. My wife refused to go out on the river ice after that episode.

Sometimes in winter a trail hidden by successive storms, or invisible in the darkness, has to be felt out step by step for miles at a time; and that at a speed little, if any less, than that attained to on good footing and during the daylight hours. The trail itself, if once passed over previously, is harder than the surrounding snow and a slight give of the shoe, slightly off on one side, is sensed, and the error rectified, without pause, at the next step. Thus a man and his outfit are enabled to pass dryshod over lakes that are often otherwise a sea of slush beneath the field of snow. A few steps into this and snowshoes and toboggan become a mass of slush which immediately freezes, making progress impossible and involving the loss of an hour or more.[11]

But to watch ice form, like molten water, in layers streaked with organic residue, building in great terraces, bridges, and pinnacles over a waterfall is an extravagant display of winter magic. And to see this monolithic sculpture accented in morning mist and incident sunlight, brilliant, gleaming, and ostentatious, is to revel in the godliness of Nature; even if you don't believe in god, you will believe in something otherworldly. The sound of the river muted under the façade of ice, faded voices of river spirits, held captive until the warm rains of April melt it away.

Ice has a particular beauty to it, moulded by inertia and gravity if from moving water over rock, while lake ice can candle into shimmering chandelier-like sceptres, chiming together under the undulating motion of the waves; and again as the formation of ice glazed on the tree branches on a cold night, mist crystallizing into jewels, ornaments and charms, dazzling the eyes in morning sunlight, disappearing all too quickly.

And to travel over a frozen lake on a cold-penetrating night, to stop under the blue blush of moon lighting the still landscape, so still you hear your heart beating and you stop walking because the squeak of leather and the crunch of snow underfoot seems too strident, and you stand on the snow-covered ice plain in the middle of the lake and just listen to night sounds — the booming of lake ice as it shifts under great pressure, and the quick-snap retort of trees popping and cracking in the extreme bitter cold as if responding in contempt for such hardship. Somewhere an owl calls, perhaps successful in its search for prey — likely a snowshoe hare, caught in a moment of fatal disregard.

And the next day, as you snowshoe toward the owl call, you follow the signature in the snow of the rabbit, from gentle pacing to frenzied

---

11   From "The Trail," by Grey Owl.

leaps until it ends abruptly in a deeply imprinted impression of owl wings, flared out in a double fan, a struggle, drops of blood in the snow, and then all traces of night business disappear entirely.

Once you get accustomed to walking or skiing over ice, you can tell a lot about its structure and thickness by the sound it makes when striking it with a ski pole or walking stick. It's almost like checking the quality of firewood by tapping it with the back of an axe — a dull thud means the wood is punky, while a sharp retort means it's solid. Ice can be gauged the same way, in most instances, and true to tell whether the ice is good or not.

If ice is covered in snow, you have no idea if it's strong enough until you test it out; and to do this it takes one step at a time and a plunge with the blade of the axe every few feet. An axe will deflect off the surface of ice if it's thick enough to hold your weight; otherwise, if an axe penetrates the ice cleanly and water surges up through the crack, it's time to back off or choose another route. One sure measure to check the security of ice, especially on rivers where there are often deadly currents, is to find fresh moose tracks that have visibly allowed the half-ton animal to make the crossing safely. There are times when deer and moose have not made crossings successfully and have succumbed in the ice water, their carcasses showing up in the river in the spring, bloated and putrefied.

Sometimes speed and foot displacement is enough to get you over thin ice, and it's happened to me on a number of occasions while winter camping. On skis you have the ability to keep up momentum until you clear the section of thin ice. I've felt myself sinking before, suddenly and quite unexpected, ski poles plunging through the thin layer of ice as water seeped up into the track behind me. Keeping up a good stride until my poles hit hard ice has pulled me out of a bind on more than one outing. Snowshoeing over thin ice can be a bit trickier; even though you are displacing more weight over a larger area than you do while skiing, you don't have the benefit of speed ... and that's when gravity works against you.

Flying in to one of my cabins in late December, my wife and I had decided to spend Christmas and New Year's in seclusion. It was an early freeze-up and only two days before Christmas, and the ice on most of the larger lakes had just formed. But from the air, I could see multiple open water holes and "soft" spots where ice had not taken yet, and we had about five kilometres to trek pulling a heavily laden toboggan. On the surface, once we started to snowshoe across the lake, the weak spots were not as visible until we were almost upon them. The first indication we had of weak ice were the wave undulations, modest but significant fluctuations on the surface.

I had seen Bear Island Anishnabai run their snow machines over the first late fall lake ice only a day after they were driving their steel boats to the mainland. Some think of it as a contest or a test of bravery, to be the first to cross the lake over the ice. And you watch them race by, ice rolling in waves behind their machines as if there were no ice at all, a thickness that would not suspend a man's weight, yet by speed alone they manage to make the crossing. Had their snowmobile lost power, even for a nanosecond, they would have plunged to their death in the deep lake. One ingenious man had tied two canoes abreast of his snow machine, like outriggers, and skimmed across any open water without the fear of crashing through.

But like any skill learned and earned in the outdoors, ice walking becomes second nature, a part of the wilderness psyche that allows one inherent freedom to go wherever one pleases. The benefit of a snow-covered landscape, or frozen lake, creek, or river, is inestimable in ease of travel and the ability to explore places one cannot outside of the season. To follow a wilderness creek valley or fenland on snowshoes in midwinter is a birder's paradise and naturalist's dream: impassable in the summer with its tangle of willow and fathomless bog, the winter trail is now smooth and free of windfall and foot-snag. Winter birds — redpolls, crossbills, rose-breasted grosbeaks, and chickadees — descend upon the flats to eat the catkin seeds off alder shrubs; otters play in the creeks where the ice hasn't congealed, their trough-like track skidding across the snow, in and out of the creek, dining areas packed down and scattered with broken clam shells and slimy carcasses of uneaten tadpoles; and browsing moose leave deep furrows, feeding off the tender shoots of moose maple and alder that grow by the forest edge.

And often, as you trek along these wintertide walkways, you will encounter magnificent granite or gneissic cliffs rising from a lake shore, ledges mounded with snow, topped with pine, and — most strikingly

— a frozen waterfall gracing its rock face, resplendent in its static form, glistening in the sun, spires of ice in multi-coloured hue.

Ice can be beautiful and dangerous, like most things in Nature, depending upon how we choose to appreciate it. Ice in a consumerist, urban environment usually means power failures, impassable roads, snow days for children, and a disruption of our standard comfort zone. We only need to change our perspective somewhat and maybe welcome the next ice storm as an opportunity to reconnect with our primitive selves and to spend time with our children.

> The one-time gloomy forest becomes cheerful in its bright mantle of snow, the
> Weight of which bears down the fanlike foliage of the evergreens, letting in the sublight, and what once were shadowed crypts becomes avenues of light.[12]

---

12   Grey Owl, from *Men of the Last Frontier*, "The Land of Shadows."

19

MOBILITY

There are many who walk through the woods like blind men.
— Grey Owl, *Tolerance*

First Nations people mimicked and adopted the movements of certain animals and birds into their own animations, for hunting, for ceremony, and for simplicity of movement through the toughest of landscapes. *Naturalizing* mobility, if you were good at it, rewarded the hunter with a successful catch; to understand the nature of Nature through tracking and being cognizant of the style of movement of game was an art all but lost through the modernization of a culture.

"You can always tell a white man from an Indian," a Native elder once told me.

"The Indian walks like a fox, in a straight line, one foot in front of the other; a white man walks with his feet pointing in opposite directions, like he wasn't sure which way to go."

This assessment intrigued me, so much so that I began watching people and how they walk, whether in a city environment or along a wilderness trail. And it was true; modern people shuffle along with their feet splayed out with an economy of effort. After all, there was no need to follow an animal trail through thick brush or to step over logs and rocks — a city landscape is predominantly flat and unexciting. Escalators have eliminated the need for steps; curbs are ramped to provide barrier-free

Ingrid Zschogner.

mobility for the challenged and, aside from dodging panhandlers, sidewalk signs, and gobs of spit, there really isn't the need to walk any differently, or the initiative to animate your movements.

As a wilderness guide, I've delved into the psychology of the adventure-seeker, as client, in such capacity as to be able to manage individuals into a group dynamic, set in a wild environment. One of the key stress-points for the occasional explorer of Nature is the challenge of mobility in a foreign landscape — to be able to walk comfortably and safely in the woods. And for some, this is often a daunting experience, one not necessarily founded on age or any particular disability other than the stigma assigned to innocence. People, generally, have lost the ability to walk like animals.

But to expect the neophyte to dance from rock to rock at a rough portage landing like a mink or an otter is an absurd probability. And because of this, mobility is often the biggest challenge for people venturing in the outdoors; and it's simply because we are not challenged enough in our daily lives. We move like domestic cows in a pasture, penned in and pampered. We have evolved into a recumbent plane of existence, shuffling, waddling, and staggering along as if lifting our feet and pointing them in the right direction was out of fashion. Perhaps it is.

A classic Canadian canoe trip usually involves paddling on lakes, interspersed with creek or river travel, and with enough obstacles thrown in to necessitate carrying your canoe and gear at regular intervals along portage trails. Yes, the much dreaded *portage!*

That slough of bog or the gauntlet of boulders that identifies a pathway contrived by some demented soul — a trail even a moose would shy away from. And the thought of having to carry all your worldly possessions on your back, *and* your mode of transportation — the canoe — has, in no small way, been cause to modify the quintessential Canadian adventure canoe trip in terms of how many portages will be encountered. Paddlers now have mutated their own aspirations of adventure by eliminating the "carry" — the fundamental and historical pith of the journey, and choose a route with the least amount of work involved.

At one time, through the three centuries of exploration and fur trade, and later during the canoe brigade days of the early 1900s, how you managed along the portage trail was the true test of a man's ability in the woods. The stress of the carry along arduous trails with two-hundred-pound loads over your back took its toll. The expected life of the voyageur was thirty-five; often dying of ruptured hernias, men pushed their bodies to the outer limit of endurance. To manage Herculean loads over rocky trails and over bottomless stretches of peat bog, dancing along wet logs, ducking through deadfall, daring not to drop your load or stop until you've reached the end of the trail, all demanded the surefooted-ness of a mountain goat.

But how do you get to that point where balance and gravity meld, and the duress of uneven ground tempts and taunts the walker of the woods, and we can move forward toward the dark forest without fear of tumbling. How does one learn to walk on the un-walkable; to manoeuvre through the forest like an animal, to balance precariously on one leg, all the while loaded down with pack and canoe, stepping up or down over ledges and fallen timber, to salsa over slick rock and mossy tree root? It's not easy.

I remember one unforgettable trip guiding two young children and their parents — a Jewish family who had little experience in the outdoors, but wanted to learn how to canoe-camp. Although the father and kids adapted well to the hard work, the mom complained bitterly and incessantly about how hard it was to portage. After four days of grumbling, the rest of the family had had enough of mom. Carrying the canoe across one rather bog-filled portage trail, I led the best way through the mire for the family to follow close behind. When we reached the end of the trail, the mom was missing.

"Oh, she's back at the beginning," one of the kids informed me.

"What's she doing?" I asked, somewhat timidly.

"She's stuck in the bog," the father said with a smirk on his face. They all began laughing hysterically.

"Mom can't get out. She yelled at us to help but we all said no ... not until she stopped complaining. So we left her there." More laughter.

I recited a story about a big bull moose, master of the forest, who could run gracefully through the thickest of bush, waving his giant head back and forth to manoeuvre through the maze of trees, and without slowing his pace, ran out onto a soft bog and sank to his belly. Unable to extricate himself, the more he struggled, the deeper he sank into the bog. Before he died of thirst, wolves had arrived to feast on the soft, exposed flanks. Unlike the moose, the wolves with their wide paws could float above the muskeg without sinking. It was a horrible death for the moose.

On hearing this account, the family ran back to the beginning of the portage to rescue their mother from the muskeg. And there she was, pack still over her shoulders, sunk to her behind in greasy mud, unable to move, lamenting the fact that her family had left her there to die. Tears and apologies, and then more laughter; even the mom joined in, and she didn't complain about portaging for the rest of the trip.

People often ask me what they should wear on their feet before embarking on a wilderness trip. The marketplace is rife with footwear geared to the outdoor trade, and it's interesting that many people opt to choose the style that least protects their feet. The trendy and infamous open-toed sandal, for some obtuse reason, has become the choice of footwear for the practicing adventurer. I won't allow these on my expeditions, except for use around the campsite; and this decision was founded on the severity of injuries, like crushed toes while wading or lining canoes up or down rapids. Hiking boots are too stiff and cumbersome, while running shoes offer little ankle protection. And what works for me isn't necessarily going to be the panacea for others looking to make walking in the wilderness any easier.

Gumboots, I tell them. *Gumboots? What the hell are they?* Made by L.L. Bean in the States, they've been around for ages. High leather tops with rubber bottoms and a chain-link tread. And my clients buy them; and I grieve over the fact that I haven't collected a royalty on the sale of Bean boots over the years, or even get a free pair mailed to me at Christmas.

Even still, regardless of the footwear, many people still have trouble navigating through the woods and along rocky portages. Inexperience, poor judgment, bad depth perception, weak knees, all make it problematic for those would-be explorers. And it gets down to the fact that walking in the wilderness is an art. Gumboots or not, the ease of travel over uneven ground rests entirely on your ability to recognize exactly the footfall locations at every step; like looking at a topographical map — if you don't follow your progress at every key reference point, you could get lost; and if you don't watch where you put each footstep, you could end up on your back like a turtle, squirming, with your pack underneath, trying to roll back over.

Even if you're good at walking on your feet, there are still those who defy sensibility while portaging by hanging small packs over their chests, obscuring the view of the trail ahead. Or those who tie in extraneous gear to their canoe, the slightest off-weight causing undue hardship for the carrier. And then there is the plastic-bag camper who packs gear into garbage bags and multiple small sacks instead of one consolidated gear bag, and stumbles and careens on and off the trail trying to drag his belongings behind. Those who pack too much in one bag, struggling to even get the pack on their back; others who try to carry more than they can physically accomplish, collapsing after a few metres; and many who carry too little, so that it takes all day to get the gear across to the end of the portage trail. And if the trail has not been maintained, then progress is slow and effort is taxed by stepping over or crawling under deadfall, dropping your load and putting it back on, bushwhacking around uprooted trees, circumnavigating flooded beaver ponds, and getting whipped in the face with brush that gets snagged on your canoe or packs. Yet another reason for the modern voyageur to steer away from old canoe route trails and keep to the beaten paths where park rangers are retained to pander to the needs of the outdoor crowd.

It's not easy to master, walking over the back of Mother Nature. I feel compassion for those learning to walk anew, like toddlers, for the first time, knees stiffening and ankles slipping, gripping at rocks that move underfoot and are covered with a primordial slime and wet moss; one wrong or misplaced step and it's a back-wrenching tumble under load, and you curse the ground you try to walk on. I warn them where to walk, where to place their feet; not to walk on the roots of trees that parallel the trail, or on a slanted rock, to keep the toes pointing forward, to register each next step before it's placed. Then, if the trail gets hard, if there is muskeg, or steep ledge, or fallen tree, and you hear the client exhale in frustration, you confirm that the trail ends just over the rise. It's a lie, and you suffer the abuse of castigation, but the client breathes easier, eventually, when they feel the breeze from the lake and they know the trail will drop gradually to the water's edge and the load will feel lighter and the pain will stop.

Even before ever reading Grey Owl's depiction of the portage in "The Lost Brigade," as a youth I had endured countless difficult portages travelled by the young Belaney in Temagami. Still, those words, eloquent and vivid, depict a facet of a way of life that bonds toil with the love of place:

> On the portages the leaves hang limp and listless, and the still air is acrid with the resinous odour of boiling spruce gum. Here men sweat under enormous burdens: earlier in the summer, clouds of mosquitoes and black-flies would envelope them in biting swarms. But it is August, and the fly season is over, and those that are left are too weak to do any damage, and sit balefully regarding us from nearby limbs of trees. Pattering of moccasined feet on the narrow trail, as men trot with the canoes, one to a man, or step easily along and under their loads; and in a miraculously short space of time everything is over to the far side.

The dreaded portage — those are the trails held in high esteem by the critics as being iniquitous and debilitating: the historic ten-mile Grand Portage that bypassed the chutes and cascades of the Pigeon River westward out of Fort William; Saskatchewan's gruelling twelve-mile Methye Portage, marking the height of land between the Hudson Bay and Arctic watersheds; the Indian Portage on the Quebec side of the Ottawa River, two miles uphill all the way to Lac Kipawa. And, as is often the case, the most arduous trails are the shorter ones.

Temagami has its fair share of difficult trails; there are more bones shattered and broken along the notorious "golden staircase" portages of the Lady Evelyn River than any other I have known. Precipitous, craggy slopes, slick rock, loose rock, crevasses and canyons, beautiful landscape graced with the most striking waterfalls but noted most for its legendary portages. I've seen young teenage boys, weighted down with heavy

Ingrid Zschogner.

wannigans on their backs, teary-eyed but stoic, climbing these trails with such pride in their hearts, stumbling, getting back up on shaky legs, prompted by canoe-mates and guides to reach the top, and to shout with glee at an accomplishment well-earned. The light-footedness of youth and a summer's tripping allows them to be nimble over rough trails.

As Grey owl wrote in "The Land of Shadows," "Beautiful as this Arctic forest appears in the daytime, it is only by moonlight, when much traveling is done to avoid the cutting winds of the daylight hours, that the true witchery of the winter wilderness grips the imagination."

I learned to travel at night when I was fourteen years old and had lost, by then, any residual fear of the dark. I would run in the dead of night for miles, through fields, down farmer's laneways and the bush trails near my home, training my eyes to see shapes and gauge distances, and ski by moonlight — *mahingan webedah* — wolf tooth. Wolves travel by night. And so it is that the ability to travel at night, like the wolf, has always been a guiding principle in my life.

The necessity to travel, at times, if not encumbered by three-day blizzard or slow-moving summer storm, will avail itself by moving at night. Winds calm at sunset and skies often clear, the signal obvious for a night ski or snowshoe, or a paddle down a large lake that, by day, has whipped up powerful whitecaps, making it impossible to make any headway at all. Those who have travelled with me on many a Canadian river well know that a night paddle is part and parcel of the itinerary, whether by need or by force of habit, or simply for the mystique of it; to drift silently on the current in slow circles, gazing heavenward at the stars or the spectral lights of the Dance of the Deadmen, smoke a pipe and cup your hands around the bowl to warm your hands, the miles slide by before you know it.

I have drifted the length of a full days paddle at night on many occasions, or crossed a lake on glass-water with only the stars illuminating the way, and a thin line of trees barely visible on the horizon. I've sailed by night down the coast of Hudson Bay just to take advantage of the tide. Night mobility is not about tempting fate, or necessarily something that is done to push the clock, however; some progression is required while on the trail.

Grey Owl— *Wa-sha-quon-asin* — knew the efficacy of night travel better than most:

> There is a peculiar, indescribable charm attached to night journeying that is handed down to some of us from the dawn of time; few can realize, without the experience, the feeling of wilderness and barbaric freedom that possesses the soul of one who travels alone in the dark, out on the edge of the world ...

AFTERWORD

There is no question about the extent to which Archie Belaney, aka Grey Owl, aka Wa-sha-quon-asin, suffered internally. In today's terms and behavioural patternology, Grey Owl may have been labelled a sociopath, or as having DPD — dissocial personality disorder.

Archie made up his life as it unfolded, often fabricating events and traits that suited his personal discretion or how he wanted to be perceived by others. He went to great lengths to convince people that he was an Indian, most likely because he couldn't survive within the conscribes of the white man's world; he found it easier to hide behind the ruse.

Taken away from his notoriety, Archie Belaney was uncontrollable; challenged by authority, or by love, he didn't have the capacity to understand the veracity behind his recalcitrant actions. He lacked remorse, unless it served his egoistic goals; and the question arises whether he truly believed in what he was doing for the benefit of conservation, or to serve some altruistic facet of his personality. I see this all the time happening in the ranks of the environmental elite.

For Archie, the ruse had to be fed constantly, and to do this Grey Owl played the part exquisitely. This transpired during a time of economic despair; the Great Depression had rooted itself into the psyche and pockets of several nations, yet, surprisingly, the National Parks of Canada opened its coffers to provide Grey Owl fuel to feed the deception.

For Canada and Great Britain, Grey Owl was a hero when they needed one, and he epitomized, quite easily, the believable figure of the Indian persona, regardless of his striking blue eyes, tall stature, and command of the English language with which he could whisk the audience away to the Land of Shadows by the use of eloquent metaphors and descriptive passages. After all, who but a true Indian could possibly know these things?

Beyond the fact that he was a failed father, husband, and lover, and lied to the world about who he was, there is the greater truth in all of this: Archie Belaney, by whatever influences, brought the message of conservation to the world. From a purely Machiavellian perspective, *the end does justify the means.* This philosophy has been used almost extensively by the modern environmental movement and by the forces that reign dominion over Canada's resources. The green movement has seen unscrupulous tactics used by both camps to gain public favour.

Grey Owl actually began to believe in himself and in the power he wielded from his notoriety. His greatest frustration, despite his popularity, was his unpopularity at home, and by the loss of his true love — Anahareo. He could manipulate, manage, control, and entertain outsiders with such grace, charm, and personal magnetism, yet he could not manage his affairs at home. To his peers, associate park wardens, his foiled relationships, and even to his children, he was "Archie Baloney," a target of disrespect. And this was due to his actions and temperament. The greater his successes, the deeper he fell into a deep funk about his identity. I believe he wanted to die before people found out. And there was also the underlying possibility that, once he had removed himself from the scene, people would quickly forget about the good things he had accomplished, and the thought of failing, even at that, paralyzed him. Certainly, the Prince Albert Park officials expected the public to forget about Grey Owl, but they never did, and his reputation as a conservationist survived the scandal. His malfeasant obsessions and dark side simply made him a more colourful character.

For a man who lived a multifarious outdoor life, of trapper, guide, mail carrier, and park ranger, Archie depended on his own physical prowess for survival in the worst of environmental conditions. For all intent and purposes, Archie was the quintessential "survivor man," and he lived often by the skin-of-his-teeth. And if I were to choose a quote from the man that best suits his moral fibre and deviationist leanings, I would most certainly use one from "Comfort" in *Tales of an Empty Cabin*. Whereupon having to shave, with a hunting knife, a frozen bannock during a winter blizzard, and losing some of the bits, Grey Owl remarked that "he would as soon have thrown away a bucket of diamonds." Having personally been in this situation, when life on the trail stretches thin the fabric of a man's fortitude, wealth — by any definition — relates to what best resolves an immediate problem in the backwoods under stressful conditions.

Being ensconced within the confines of the National Park system drove the man to near madness. Having to conform to a rather stringent bureaucratic protocol wasn't in Archie's makeup; for him it was like forced retirement with strings attached ... and he was the performing puppet. His health was suffering: war injuries compromised his stamina; his lungs were weaker, feet often swollen; it was likely he suffered from osteoporosis. I can attest to the level of depreciation the body suffers after years of physical hardship. Kneeling in a canoe was probably difficult for the aging Grey Owl, and once-simple tasks, like hoisting a canoe over his shoulders, would have to be done with utmost caution so as not to exacerbate weakening discs and frayed cartilage. While filming his hallmark river adventure on the Mississaga, Grey Owl had to relinquish the stern of his canoe to a lesser paddler; Archie couldn't manage the canoe efficiently because he probably found it too painful to kneel properly. Beneath the charming smiles and the virtual ease with which he manoeuvred his canoe in front of enthralled tourists, Archie was most likely hiding a lot of deep-set pain. The guide's mantra did not allow a visibly weak exterior to show at anytime; to be true to his writings, Owl had to maintain the visage of the tireless man in his stories. After three knee operations, I can no longer dance like an otter over the river rocks; my balance is precarious under a load, and my abilities have been severely compromised. It has been a personal source of consternation and disappointment that I can no longer keep up the pace I was accustomed to. Grey Owl felt the miles on the trail creeping up; the only sense of gratification, for Owl, was to live vicariously again through his stories, boosted by copious amounts of scotch. Any interruptions would be met with stern retribution. He knew he was losing hold on his life and perhaps his purpose; failing health, unrequited love, a deception soon to be revealed, and the uncertainty that even the good things he accomplished would be forgotten by those who felt jilted by the ruse.

And Grey Owl wasn't the first famous impostor. There was Chief Buffalo Child Long Lance (1890–1932), born Sylvester Clark Long, an American journalist from Carolina who gained international prominence as a spokesman for Native causes. Claiming Blackfoot and Cherokee blood, he even fought with the Canadian Expeditionary Force in France during the First World War and was wounded twice. After the war he claimed full-blood Blackfoot lineage, wrote and lectured about the Plains Indians, and produced the noted film *Silent Enemy* — an epic of the American Indian. He was eventually branded as a fraud.

There was Forrest Carter (1925–79), born Earl Carter, who claimed to be Cherokee after reinventing himself. He was a bigot and speechwriter for Governor George Wallace of Alabama. His claim to fame was twofold: an epic book and movie entitled *The Education of Little Tree,* and the founding of a paramilitary Ku Klux Klan splinter group. And, more recently, Nasdijj, or Tomothy Patrick Barrus (1950–), one of the best examples of a man whose memoirs were published under false titles and lineage.

But Archie Belaney was different; he believed in a cause that really meant something to people. It was the draw of the hinterland trail that became surrogate parents to Archie, and those who dwelled in the Land of Shadows, both human and animal, that taught him to respect the ways of the wilderness. This was not a lifestyle contrived on a part-time whim, as it is with so many self-seekers. Archie embraced the trail life with such zeal and effort that it made it possible for him, as a writer and lecturer, to be the voice of the wilderness; it was Archie's *real* love, over and above everything and anyone else in his life. Grey Owl was the product of Archie Belaney's genius. Undeniably, they were both men of passion, in love and life, with expectations that were destined to dry up as ephemeral pools. Expecting that his young love would stay by his side through thick or thin was a gross misjudgment. Anahareo outgrew Archie. Archie was caught up in a cesspool of guilt and depression and drink. But the legend lives on, in his stories and in his protracted life.

He died in the month of April — the "patches of earth, developing sun" moon, *baubaukunaetae-geezis*. Perhaps it is reflective of his "patchy" character and deeds that "shine" through adversity and scandal.

> *The feel of a canoe gunnel at the thigh, the splash of flying spray in the face, the rhythm of the snowshoe trail, the beckoning of far-off hills and valleys, the majesty of the tempest, the calm and silent presence of the trees that seem to muse and ponder in their silence; the trust and confidence of small living creatures, the company of simple men; these have been my inspiration and guide. Without them I am nothing.*
>
> — Wa-sha-quon-asin (Grey Owl), 1888–1938

BIBLIOGRAPHY

Chapter 1: Quote from Paul Watson used by permission (*seashepherd.org*).

Chapter 7: Revised Script, *Grey Owl*, by William Nicholson, January 27, 1998, Beaver Productions Ltd., Surrey, England.

Chapter 16: Hutchens, Alma R., *Indian Herbalogy of North America*. Berkeley, CA: Shambhala Publications Inc., 1973.

Grey Owl Quotes Used

Grey Owl. *The Men of the Last Frontier*, Paperback Edition. Toronto: Stoddart Publishing, 1992 (originally published in 1931 by Macmillan of Canada).

Grey Owl. *Pilgrims of the Wild*, Paperback Edition. London: Puffin Books: A Division of Penguin Books Ltd., 1973 (First published in 1935).

Grey Owl. *Stories of the Early Days in Canada's North: Tales of an Empty Cabin*, Paperback Edition. Toronto: Stoddart Publishing, 1992 (originally published in 1936 by Macmillan of Canada).

Reference Only

Henry, Michael, and Peter Quinby. *Ontario's Old-Growth Forests.*
    Markham, ON: Fitzhenry & Whiteside, 2010.
Ruffo, Armand Garnet. *Grey Owl: The Mystery of Archie Belaney.* Regina:
    Coteau Books, 1996.

ABOUT THE AUTHOR

A self-taught artist and photographer, **Hap Wilson** has travelled over sixty thousand kilometres by canoe and snowshoe, and embarked on more than three hundred wilderness expeditions. He is one of North America's best-known wilderness guides and canoeists, and has been building sustainable trails for more than thirty years. He is also the co-founder of the environmental group Earthroots. He lives in Rosseau, Ontario. For more information, please visit Hap's website at *www.eskakwa.ca.*

ABOUT THE ILLUSTRATOR

Ingrid Zschogner is self-taught artist and outdoor enthusiast who has been creating detailed portraits in oil, graphite, and pastel for more than fifteen years. She is also a professional trailbuilder, wilderness guide, and environmental activist. To view Ingrid's portfolio, please visit her website at *www.wildrosedesigns.ca.*

ALSO BY HAP WILSON

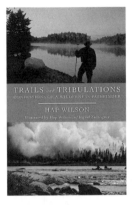

Trails and Tribulations
Confessions of a Wilderness Pathfinder
978-1-55488-397-4
$26.99 / £15.99

In an age when "survival" shows permeate the media, noted northern traveller Hap Wilson shares accounts of his lifelong involvement with wilderness living on the Canadian Shield. *Trails and Tribulations* takes the reader on a journey with the author through natural settings ranging from austere to mysterious and breathtaking. Experience animal attacks, bush fires, the threat of hypothermia, and the wonder of Native vision-quest sites in this truly remarkable adventure.

The Cabin
A Search for Personal Sanctuary
978-1-89704-505-3
$24.95 / US$19.95 / £17.50

A century ago, a young doctor from Cleveland, Robert Newcomb, travelled north to Temagami. It was as far north as one could travel by any modern means. Beautiful beyond any simple expletive, the Temagami wilderness was rich in timber, clear-water lakes, fast flowing rivers, mystery, and adventure. Bewitched by the spirit of an interior river, the Majamagosibi, Newcomb had a remote cabin built overlooking one of her precipitous cataracts. The cabin remained unused for decades, save for a few passing canoeists; it changed ownership twice and slowly began to show its age. The author discovered the cabin while on a canoe trip in 1970. Like Newcomb, Hap Wilson was lured to Temagami in pursuit of adventure and personal sanctuary. That search for sanctuary took the author incredible distances by canoe and snowshoe, through near death experiences and Herculean challenges. Wilson finally became owner of The Cabin in 2000.

OF RELATED INTEREST

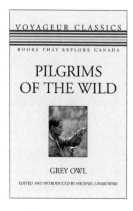

Pilgrims of the Wild
Grey Owl
978-1-55488-734-7 $26.99 £15.99

First published in 1935, *Pilgrims of the Wild* is Grey Owl's autobiographical account of his transition from successful trapper to conservationist. With his Iroquois wife Anahareo, Grey Owl set out to protect the environment and the endangered beaver. Powerful in its simplicity, it tells the story of Grey Owl's life of happy cohabitation with the wild creatures of nature and the healing powers of what he referred to as "the great Northland" of "Over the Hills and Far Away."

Available at your favourite bookseller.

DUNDURN PRESS
w w w . d u n d u r n . c o m

What did you think of this book?
Visit www.dundurn.com for reviews, videos, updates, and more!